AF616566

A REPORT
ON THE 1931 POWELL MOUND EXCAVATIONS, MADISON COUNTY, ILLINOIS

by

Steven R. Ahler
University of Kentucky
Lexington, Kentucky[1]

and

Peter J. DePuydt
University of Wisconsin
Milwaukee, Wisconsin[2]

Illinois State Museum
Reports of Investigations, No. 43
Springfield, Illinois
1987

Current Addresses:
[1]Illinois State Museum
Springfield, Illinois 62706

[2]303 E. Frederick St.
Lancaster, Pennsylvania 17602

1987
ISSN 0360-0270
ISBN 0-89792-111-9
Printed by Authority
of the State of
Illinois

CONTENTS

LIST OF FIGURES

LIST OF TABLES

ACKNOWLEDGEMENTS

This report could not have been written without the help of a number of individuals. Of these people, we would like to especially thank Bonnie W. Styles of the Illinois State Museum for graciously lending the Powell Mound collection to the University of Wisconsin--Milwaukee (UWM). Melvin L. Fowler, who saw the need for a report on this material, arranged for the Powell Mound material to be available to us. His knowledge and experience with the site of Cahokia were very informative in the course of analysis. We would also like to thank Charles Bareis of the University of Illinois for lending us the original field notes taken by Thorne Deuel. Comments by anonymous reviewers were helpful in the final editing of the manuscript for publication.

At UWM, many friends and colleagues freely gave us their time and advice during the washing, labelling, and identification steps of the project. Barbara Vander Leest, Elizabeth Benchley, and David Graham helped greatly in the identification of the ceramic assemblage. Mary Jo Staggs of the University of Kentucky provided the artifact drawings and sherd profiles. Numerous individuals spent more than one afternoon washing and labelling the material, and we would like to thank the following: Marcia Birong-Koenen, William Horstman, Connie Horstman, Greg James, Dennis Kolb, Michael Kolb, Diane Lehman, Michele Patin-James, Lynne Peters-Sullivan, Roland Rodell, James Stark, Pam Zager, and Steve Zager.

A REPORT ON THE 1931 POWELL MOUND EXCAVATIONS, MADISON COUNTY, ILLINOIS

INTRODUCTION

The Powell Mound in the American Bottom was once one of the largest structures in the Cahokia mound group, exceeded in size only by Monks Mound. It was located at the western boundary of the Cahokia group at the present site of the Venture discount store at the junction of Illinois State Highway 111 and US Route 40, about 2.6 km (1.6 miles) due west of Monks Mound (see Figure 1).

During February 1931, Thorne Deuel of the University of Chicago undertook salvage excavation in the lower portions of Powell Mound. The materials recovered from these excavations, along with other material donated by Paul F. Titterington, have since been stored at the Illinois State Museum in Springfield. In January 1980, these materials were loaned to the University of Wisconsin--Milwaukee for analysis as part of a seminar in advanced archaeological analysis conducted by Melvin L. Fowler. This report provides a descriptive account of the 1931 excavations and the salvaged material and ties these materials to the general cultural and historical development of the Cahokia site. The report is thus basically descriptive.

With the recent archaeological work conducted in the American Bottom in conjunction with the FAI-270 highway project (see Bareis and Porter [1984] and references therein), the authors felt that it would be timely and appropriate for the Powell Mound analysis to receive wider distribution than a class paper could provide. The report presented here was prepared in 1980 based on the general knowledge of the American Bottom ceramic assemblages known at that time. Only minor revisions have been made in the original paper.

BACKGROUND INFORMATION AND HISTORICAL CONSIDERATION

The Powell Mound was recorded by J. R. R. Patrick on his original map of the Cahokia site in 1876 but was not numbered at the time. Moorehead (1923, 1929) evidently misinterpreted this portion of Patrick's map and assigned the number 46 to the Powell Mound. Many later workers retained this number for the Powell Mound, though it had been clearly assigned to a different mound on Patrick's map. Fowler (n.d.) assigned the number 86 to the Powell Mound, based on a continuation of the Patrick map and on historical considerations of work at Cahokia. Though this number is more appropriate, the 1931 collections were referenced with the number 11Ms°46, which was retained for this paper.

Evidently Moorehead did not excavate into the Powell Mound, but he did record its dimensions. His records indicate that it was a ridge-top mound with a rectangular base; the long (east-west) dimension was 310 feet (94.5 m) while the north-south axis measured 170 feet (51.8 m). Its long axis was oriented on a bearing of N 89° W (Moorehead 1929:84). Other dimensions were given by Patrick as 300 x 150 feet (91.4 x 45.7 m). Titterington (1938:15) recorded the dimensions as 310 and 180 feet (94.5 x 54.9 m). Elevations for the mound were also recorded and were fairly consistent through time. Patrick in 1876 recorded an elevation of 45 feet (13.7 m), whereas Moorehead's 1929 data indicate a height of 40 feet (12.2 m). The general uniformity of reported dimensions indicates that the mound was not significantly altered, and in

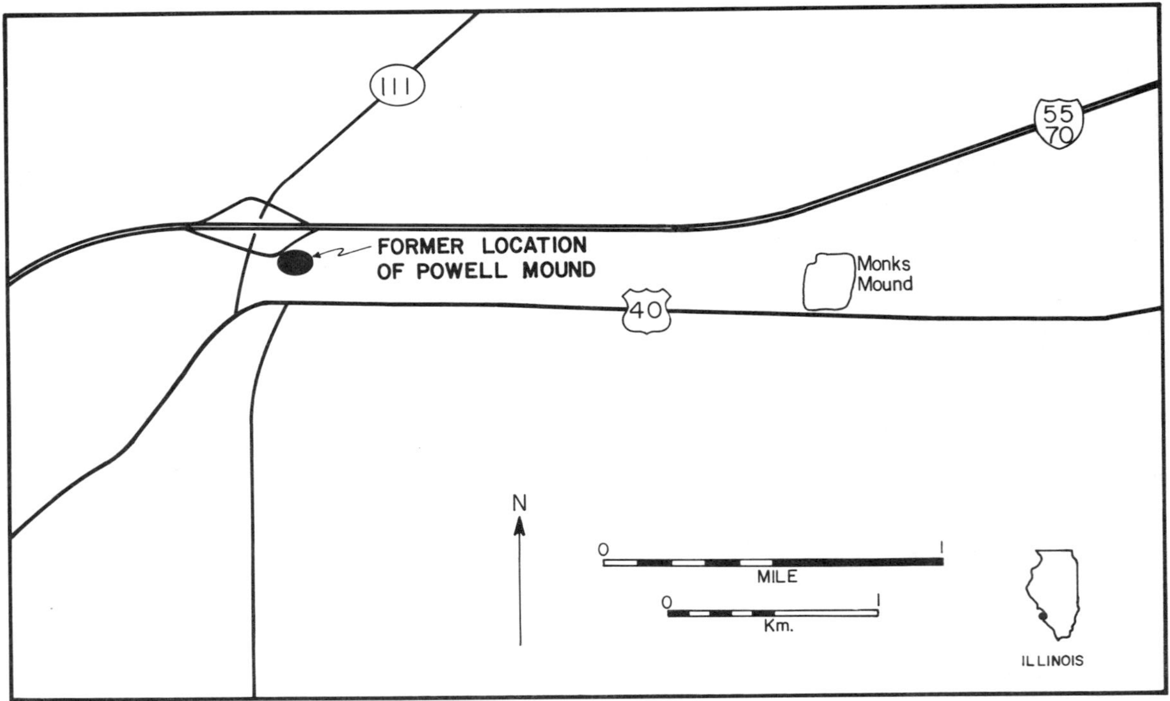

Figure 1. Location of the Powell Mound in the American Bottom, Illinois. Source map is the USGS Monks Mound 7.5' quadrangle.

1930 still probably retained its original shape and size as suggested by Titterington (1938:14). Since it had not been actively cultivated, the mound probably sustained little damage from agriculture.

During the late 1920s, William and Frederick Powell, the owners of the Powell Mound, had a standing offer of $3,000 in financial support for any scientific institution that would excavate the large mound. The offer was prefaced with only one condition--the backdirt from such excavations must be removed and used to fill a low swampy area to the north of the mound. Despite the financial stimulus, the job was apparently too big for any institution to accept the project. The state of Illinois was unwilling to purchase the entire farm, and the Powell brothers were unwilling to sell only the mound portion of their land. With this impasse, the owners decided to level the mound to place the entire farm under cultivation and began to excavate with heavy machinery in December 1930. A substantial portion of the mound was razed before anyone became aware of the activities largely because they began excavations on the side of the mound away from observation from US Route 40. Even more of the mound was destroyed before an archaeological observer could be present.

In late December 1930, A. R. Kelley of the University of Illinois was sent to act as observer; scientific hand excavations were permitted as long as these did not interfere with the contractor's schedule (Titterington 1938:14, Kelley 1933, Kelley and Cole 1931). Present also at the razing was Paul F. Titterington, an amateur archaeologist from St. Louis whose on-site observations during the razing are invaluable for interpreting the mound's internal structure. Titterington also made notes of the excavations, provided sketches of various points of interest, and collected a variety of materials from the mound during its destruction. Many of these specimens were later donated to the Illinois State Museum and are incorporated into the present analysis.

GENERAL OBSERVATIONS

Several important observations were made by both Kelley and Titterington during the destruction of the mound. The following statements are collectively compiled from Titterington (1938), Kelley (1933), and Kelley and Cole (1931).

One of the most distinctive features of the mound was its internal structure. The steam shovel used to excavate the mound provided opportunities to observe cross sections through both major and minor axes. Titterington (1938:Fig. 47) showed a photograph of the major axis of the mound taken by A. J. Meyers (Figure 2). Clearly visible is a dark line about halfway down the profile. This line represented the probable humus level associated with an early major construction stage of the mound. The line configuration in both cross sections indicates that the earlier mound had the shape of the familiar truncated pyramid, common to Middle Mississippian sites. These mounds are more common at Cahokia than are the linear ridge-top mounds (Fowler n.d.). This earlier major construction stage used sediments composed of the black gumbo clay that makes up a large part of the topsoil horizons in the American Bottom. The distinct humus line noted at the top of this construction stage was observed to be about four inches thick. This thickness suggests that the mound surface was stable for a sufficient length of time to permit soil horizonation to begin or to allow a moderate accumulation of organic debris through human occupation. Above the humus line is the last major construction

Figure 2. Powell Mound during destruction in January 1931. The view is from the northeast, showing the original mound shape and the dark organic surface forming the top and sides of the lower major pyramidal mound (episode 6). The figure is reproduced from a print on file at the Illinois State Museum; the original negative is on file with Charles J. Bareis, University of Illinois. Originally published in Titterington (1938:Figure 47).

stage. This stage employed sediments that were lighter in color and composed of more silty and sandy soils than the lower construction stage. These sediments are commonly found underlying the darker gumbo surface soils in the American Bottom. The completion of this last major construction stage gave the mound its historically recorded shape, that of a rounded linear ridge-top mound.

At the interface between the two major construction stages, two large rectangular burial pits were observed. One was located about one-third of the way into the mound from its western edge but was completely destroyed by the machinery. The other was about one-third of the way into the mound from its eastern edge and was partially excavated by the University of Illinois observers. This feature proved to be a rectangular pit measuring about 20 by 30 feet (6.1 x 9.1 m). Parallel cedar sticks had been laid flat on the bottom of the pit and covered with a layer of bark. Human burials were then placed, extended, on the bark layer and covered with one to five layers of small shell beads. These shells (*Marginella* sp.) were found in parallel rows over the bones, indicative of a shell blanket or mat. All were also cut or ground at the proximal end, presumably to facilitate stringing. Superimposed upon the shell layer was another layer of bark. Other intentionally included grave goods were present, including shell necklaces and copper-covered cedar ornaments. Some of these burial materials were collected by Titterington and the University of Illinois observers. Most of these specimens were available for study, as well as some pertinent field notes made by Titterington.

Also at the surface of the first major mound stage, a large upright cedar post was observed. The post was broken, but was at least 18 inches (46 cm) long, extending down into the lower mound. It was located slightly west of the center of the mound. This description is reminiscent of other large post pits and post remains found elsewhere in the vicinity of Cahokia. Large post pits, some with post remains intact, have been observed at Mound 72 (Fowler and Hall 1972), on the southwestern corner of Monks Mound (Fowler n.d.), and at the Mitchell site north of Cahokia proper (Porter 1974).

The two burial pits and the large post form a straight line oriented slightly north of due west, very similar to the orientation of the final shape of the Powell Mound. Extending this straight line to the east intersects the southwestern corner of Monks Mound on the first terrace (Figure 3) at or near the location

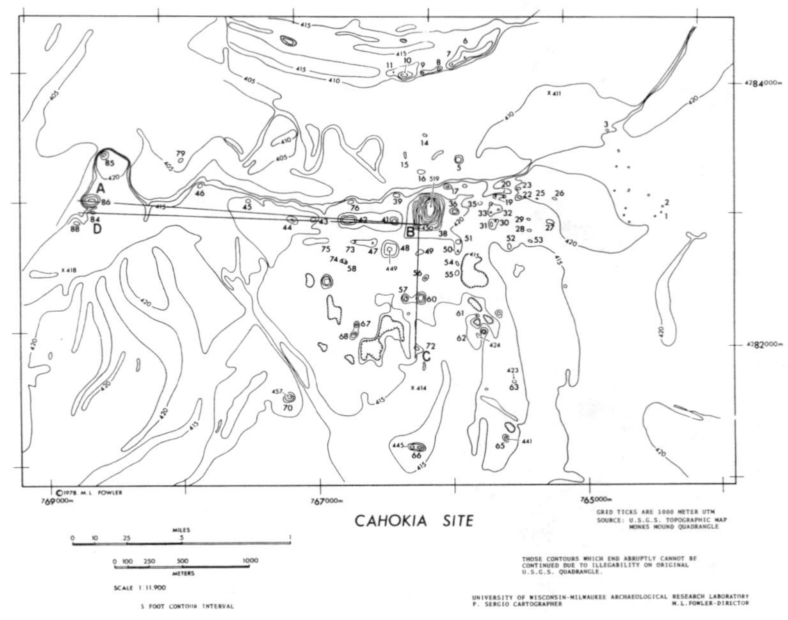

Figure 3. Location of the Powell Mound (A, number 86) in relation to other mounds at Cahokia. Location B is a low conical mound on the southwestern corner of the first terrace of Monks Mound; location C is Mound 72; Location D is Mound 84. Angle ABC is 92°; angle DBC is 90°. (Figure reproduced courtesy of University of Wisconsin--Milwaukee Archaeological Research Laboratories.) For enlargement of figure see page 38.

of the large post pit mentioned above. This structured orientation indicates that the Powell Mound was incorporated into the overall geographic orientation of the Cahokia site at least as early as the first major construction stage of the mound and possibly much earlier. Mound 84, located immediately south of the Powell Mound, may also be important in the general orientation of mounds at Cahokia. A line drawn from this mound to the east intersects several other mounds before also intersecting Monks Mound at the southwestern corner of the first terrace. A right angle turn to the south from this point would intersect Mound 72. Mound 84, though small in comparison to other mounds at Cahokia, may be more important than the Powell Mound for marking internal site structure.

In general, little material was recovered from the Powell Mound during the razing. The leveling of the mound was halted in January 1931, and at that time only occasional items of interest had been salvaged. Most of the salvaged material available for study and incorporated into this report was recovered from the general mound fill and the burial areas by Titterington. When the razing was halted, the Powell Mound remained only 7 feet (2.1 m) high.

UNIVERSITY OF CHICAGO CONTROLLED EXCAVATIONS

In February 1931, the Powell brothers granted permission for controlled excavations to be conducted in the remaining basal portion of the mound. Excavations were under the direction of Thorne Deuel of the University of Chicago in coordination with W. C. McKern of the Milwaukee Public Museum. The results of these excavations were not comprehensively reported, but again Titterington (1938), Kelley (1933), and Kelley and Cole (1931) all provided partial accounts. As before, the following is compiled from these partial records, and additional information was obtained from the field notes taken by Deuel.

Excavations began on 6 February 1931 in the basal 7 feet (2.1 m) of the mound. Unfortunately, the field notes for the initial period of excavation were not available. A single book of field notes labelled "Book #2" was loaned to us by Charles Bareis of the University of Illinois. It is assumed that the first notebook in this set has been either lost or misplaced in the years since the excavations took place. Copies of the Book #2 notes now reside with the material collections at the Illinois State Museum. The actual description of field techniques and grid/elevation systems were not explicitly included in Book #2, but are reconstructed below from sketches and other indirect information included in the available notes. The Illinois State Museum also provided a partial catalog of excavated material, which helped to clarify the provenience information.

Apparently, relatively standard University of Chicago field techniques were employed by Deuel. Figure 4 depicts the reconstructed excavation plan. Two main trenches were excavated through the mound. An east-west trench was placed through the major axis; a north-south trench was excavated perpendicular to and generally bisecting the east-west trench. The east-west trench is over 300 feet (91.4 m) long, whereas the north-south trench exceeds 200 feet (61.0 m) in length. All trenches were segmented into 5 x 10 foot (1.5 x 3.0 m) units. The unit designation apparently refers to the southwestern corner of each excavation unit. Excavation units are labeled xxxLyyy or xxxRyyy, with "xxx" designating the number of feet grid north of an arbitrary O/O point and "yyy" designating the number of 10-foot (3.0 m) excavation units to the west or east of the north-south running center line, respectively. Excavation units are 10 feet (3.0 m) in length, so that R3 would have its southwestern corner 30 feet (9.1 m) east of the center line. Grid north evidently corresponds to magnetic north.

The north-south trench was excavated with its western profile on the R1 line, 10 feet (3.0 m) east (right) of the center line. The major east-west trench was placed between the 100 and 105 (north) lines. Two shorter trenches were also excavated in a north--south direction, crossing the main trench. The "east cross trench" was excavated for a distance of 60 feet (18.3 m) along the R9 1/2 line (95 feet [29.0 m] east of the center line) and was 5 feet (1.5 m) wide. The "west cross trench" was placed along the L4 1/2 line and was also 5 feet (1.5 m) wide and 60 feet (18.3 m) long. Three additional units (presumably 5 x 10 feet [1.5 x 3.0 m]) were excavated southwest of the east cross trench in a northeast-southwest diagonal pattern. The orientation of these units (50R6, 60R7, and 70R8) is problematical.

Individual artifacts were often bagged separately during excavation, and in these cases unit, depth, and grid location were recorded. Provenience data were available for over 300 artifacts. The depth was referred to in the field notes as "below datum," and it is assumed that a single datum was employed for the entire excavated area. Depths below surface are not

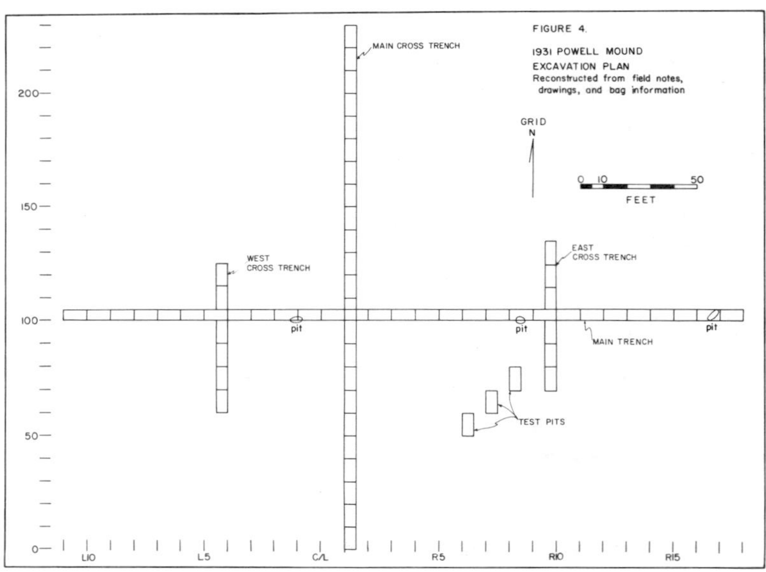

Figure 4. Reconstructed excavation plan for the University of Chicago controlled excavations at the base of Powell Mound. For enlargement of figure see page 39.

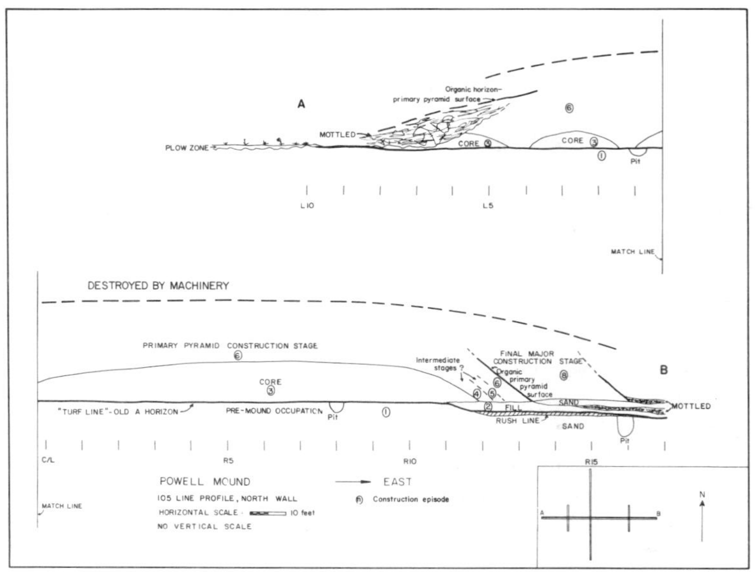

Figure 5. Reconstruction of the Main Trench east-west profile through the basal portion of the Powell Mound. Construction/activity episodes are numbered. The sources for the reconstruction information are field notes (Book #2), sketches, and bag lists. For enlargement of figure see page 40.

mentioned anywhere. The alternative possibility is that each excavation unit had a designated datum point that referenced only items within that unit. Since some of the depth measurements are recorded as positive rather than negative depths, this alternative seems unlikely. The provenience information used here assumes that a single elevation datum was used for the entire excavated area.

No scale profile drawings were available for study, but verbal descriptions and one sketch of the main trench profile were included in the Book #2 notes. The main east-west profile was reconstructed from the available information (Figure 5). This drawing can be assumed to be accurate only for relative positions of the features and strata since few horizontal and no vertical measurements were available.

The bottom of the "turf line" is generally assumed to be about 5 feet (1.5 m) below datum, as indicated in the field notes. This turf line apparently represents an intact premound organic soil horizon. To the east, this turf line dips down to approximately 5 to 6 feet (1.5-1.8 m) below its usual elevation. This area to the east was evidently an old slough or swampy area and was filled by the Cahokia inhabitants to a level comparable to the surrounding ground surface before the actual mound construction began. The mound itself was evidently constructed in several discrete episodes, with the areas marked as "core" being composed of smaller ridges or initial mounds that were later consolidated into a single platform mound. Because of their spatial separation, there is no way to determine the order of construction of these core mounds. At least one core was constructed subsequent to the filling of the low slough area, since it partially overlies the artificial fill. Core mounds were also employed as the initial construction episodes of Mound 72, a relatively small ridge-topped burial mound located southeast of Powell Mound (Fowler and Hall 1972).

The bottom of the slough contained a layer of rushes and grasses as well as a variety of ceramic artifacts. Samples of these plant remains were sent to the University of Michigan Ethnobotanical Laboratory for identification in March 1931. The specimens identified (see later section for details) included primarily sedges and grasses with traces of seeds or vegetal remains of *Chenopodium*, *Polygonum*, and *Populus* species (Gilmore n.d.). All of these species inhabit low wetlands and would be common in backwater areas that were seasonally flooded. Below the level of the vegetal remains (referred to here as the "rush line") were several artifacts including human and animal bones, ceramics, and chert debitage. Also below the artificial fill in this low area was a single rectangular pit located in unit 100R16 and originating at about 10.9 feet (3.3 m) below datum. Two additional pits were associated with the premound occupation, one in unit 100L1 and one in unit 100R8.

At least five separate mound construction episodes were described in the field notes. The three separate core mounds collectively constitute the first mound construction episode. Dashed lines in Figure 5 near the edge of the core mounds indicate at least two intermediate construction stages that are not well documented. The last two documented episodes correspond to the limits of the major construction stages noted above. At the western limits of the profile, flood damage or collapse of the major pyramidal mound is indicated by a mixture of mottled and water-laid sediments. The last major construction event is not present in this portion of the profile.

The construction and activity episodes for the Powell Mound area for which there is some documentation are summarized below. The activity episodes are numbered and are marked on the profile drawing.

1) A premound occupation of the Powell Mound area is indicated by artifactual remains incorporated into and underlying the turf line. This turf line is probably an old humus zone, com-

posed of combined A_0 and A_1 soil horizons. This premound occupation is especially evident in the eastern part of the excavations where the original ground surface slopes down into a probable slough area. Debris was dumped into the low area to the east, accumulating in and around the organic rush line horizon. Since the rush line and the turf line cannot be segregated temporally, based on the available profile drawings, they are treated here as though they were coeval. Also associated with the premound occupation are at least three submound pit features located about 80 feet (24.4 m) apart on an east-west line through the mound. These three pits evidently originate at the top of the observed turf line and may represent some of the last premound activities in the Powell Mound vicinity. These activities may be closely related to the initial mound construction activities, and the inclusion of materials from these pits in the general premound provenience may be somewhat of an arbitrary decision.

2) The low (slough) area to the west was filled using locally available sediments. Refuse debris is incorporated into the fill sediments, but no occupational surfaces or intact features were observed within this fill zone, so it is treated here as a single depositional unit.

3) At least three small ridges or primary mounds were constructed using mainly gumbo soils from the topsoil horizons available in the American Bottom. These mounds are of varying size and undetermined overall shape. At present it is not possible to determine the order of their construction, so they are included in the same construction /activity episode. The easternmost mound overlaps the fill of episode 2.

4 and 5) There is some evidence that two additional stages of mound construction resulted in either the accretion of the core mounds or the filling of the areas between them. The core mounds may have been consolidated into a single (pyramidal?) mound by the end of episode 5. Since there is little documentary evidence of these construction stages, they are treated together here.

6) Construction of the first major pyramidal mound observed during the mound razing definitely consolidated the individual core mounds into a single structure. This episode resulted in a flat mound summit approximately 27 feet (8.2 m) above the original local ground surface.

7) Burial pits, post pit construction, and other activities are associated with the stable surface of episode 6. An unknown time span is involved in this activity episode, but presumably soil horizonation was coeval with human occupation of the mound surface. During this time, redeposited (slopewash) sand and mottled silt accumulated around the base of the mound. (Episode 7 is not shown in Figure 5).

8) The final major construction episode of the mound resulted in the capping of the pyramidal structure with lighter-colored and sandier sediments. Apparently this last mound configuration remained relatively stable, but some evidence of slumping associated with either episodes 6, 7, or 8 obliterated portions of the western limits of the mound. The "hay rick" appearance of the mound is described in historical documents, and there is little evidence of sediment redeposition at the base of this construction stage.

Undoubtedly there were many more minor construction and activity episodes within the time span represented by episodes 6, 7, and 8 above, but the lack of excavation control for the upper portions of the mound precludes documentation or even speculation about these episodes. In these later episodes, only the most gross changes in mound morphology or activities are observed in contrast to the lower portions of the mound area. Nevertheless, these occupation and activity episodes provide a rough vertical and horizontal guide for the stratigraphic analysis of the available materials. Some episodes are better represented than others, and this variability in provenience quality and representation is addressed below.

During the early 1960s, additional excavations were undertaken in the basal portions of the Powell Mound by the University of Illinois under the direction of Charles Bareis. Salvage excavations were initiated because of the construction of a large discount department store at the site of the Powell Mound. Cross trenches and several systematically placed test units were excavated. It is not known whether this later work in the basal remnants of the mound revealed evidence of the location or extent of the 1931 excavations. Examination of the field maps and notes from the 1960s salvage excavations could shed valuable light on Cahokia archaeology in general and on the Powell Mound construction sequence and artifactual assemblages in particular. Additional work in the area has been conducted in the village midden deposits to the northeast of the mound since the mid 1960s. These excavations were conducted by the University of Illinois Archaeology Field School. Comparison of these later collections to the 1931 mound excavations is not attempted, and specific information on the stratigraphy or artifactual assemblages encountered in these later excavations is currently not available in published format.

PROBLEM ORIENTATION

In their summaries of the Powell Mound excavations, Kelley (1933) and Kelley and Cole (1931) proposed that the entire Powell Mound sequence, including the premound occupations, belonged to the same general time period. They referred to this period as the "bean pot culture." It was distinguished from the preceding "pure village culture" by differences in ceramic, lithic, and mortuary styles. The pure village assemblage was best represented in the premound artifacts recovered from excavations in Mound 84, located immediately south of Powell Mound and excavated in the summer of 1931 by Gene M. Stirling of the University of Illinois. Griffin (1949) later expanded upon these differences and proposed the more familiar nomenclature of the Old Village and Trappist phases.

The original interpretations of the Powell Mound sequence offered by Kelley and Cole (1931) were used here as working hypotheses to refine the otherwise descriptive study of the 1931 collections. Three major issues are addressed: (1) the temporal depth of the Powell Mound occupations, including the premound materials; (2) the chronological placement of the materials; and (3) the chronological similarity of the premound and mound fill materials. These issues were the focus of the ceramic analyses undertaken here and may allow some additional light to be shed on the general chronological and cultural sequences at Cahokia. They will be addressed through two main aspects of the ceramic assemblage--basic assemblage description and chronological-typological comparison of proveniences and activity episodes.

GENERAL RECORDING AND ANALYSIS PROCEDURES

Because of the complexity of the initial construction stages and the lack of scale plan and profile drawings for the excavations, few artifacts in the collections can be associated with a specific construction episode. For example, materials from unit 100R6, and depth of 3.6 feet (1.1 m) below datum, can potentially be associated with episode 3, 4, 5, or 6, but cannot be assigned with confidence to any single episode. Because of these ambiguities, there are limits to the kinds of provenience-dependent analyses that can be performed. Only limited and relatively gross provenience data are applicable with any degree of confidence.

It was decided that the initial analyses should focus on ceramic typology and chronology. Emphasis was placed on isolating and defining ceramic attribute combinations that might be compared to established ceramic types for the Cahokia area. This process was accomplished through a relatively complete but certainly not exhaustive analysis of the ceramics using a tree type of attribute key. After the ceramic attribute clusters were defined and compared to existing ceramic types, a provenience-dependent analysis using the portion of the collections with specific proveniences was attempted. In order to provide as complete a report as possible, the lithic and faunal assemblages were also examined and described. Some of Titterington's collections were also included as part of the analytical sample; these specimens are noted below and treated separately when appropriate.

When the materials were received at UWM, they were still enclosed in the original field bags and had not been taken from these bags since the time of excavation. Many items were not bagged, but were simply wrapped with paper that was sometimes marked with a field number. In the case of individual items, the field notes, bag front information, and bag lists provided a partial inventory of exact proveniences matched to specific items. The majority of the materials, though, were only given gross provenience designations such as "East Cross Trench"; these materials were cataloged by lot.

After washing the materials and recording the bag front and other available provenience information, all items were cataloged using either field numbers or newly assigned numbers. Each item was labeled with the site designation 11Ms°46, denoting the Powell Mound (Illinois, Madison County, mound site, number 46). At the request of the Illinois State Museum, the site number 46 was retained though there is some doubt as to the accuracy of this number (see above discussion and Fowler n.d.). A list of the catalog numbers and associated proveniences can be obtained from the Illinois State Museum or from the UWM Archaeological Research Laboratories. Finally, the original provenience data were retained for this report, without conversion to metric units. This simplifies matters since all of the original excavations and notes are in English units of measurement. Metric equivalent are provided parenthetically when appropriate.

The analyses utilized only generalized provenience data. It was established through the field notes that the original premound humus line was between 4.5 and 5.0 feet (1.4 and 1.5 m) below datum for most of the excavation area. In the eastern part, this humus line sloped down and became the rush line in the old slough area. This humus line was used to separate the collections into three gross provenience categories.

1) Premound proveniences include items with depths recorded more than 5.0 feet (1.5 m) below datum, items found in pits or depressions, and items noted as being associated with the rush line in various verbal descriptions. These include some items from the low slough area east of the R12 line. This grouping includes all materials associated with episode 1.
2) Fill proveniences are restricted to items from proveniences east of

R11 and between 5.5 and 9.5 feet (1.7 and 2.9 m) below datum. This designation corresponds to excavated areas of the prehistorically filled low slough area in the eastern part of the main east-west trench, described above as episode 2.

3) Mound matrix proveniences are those with depth recorded as less than 4.5 feet (1.4 m) below datum regardless of horizontal location. This category represents construction episodes 3 through 8, but most of the material is probably from episodes 3 through 6.

There are gaps in the provenience data included here. Items with depths between 4.5 and 5.0 feet (1.4 and 1.5 m) below datum are not assigned to any of the provenience categories because of the ambiguity involved in determining premound or mound association. The same is true for some items in the fill zone. This factor makes the following analyses more conservative, but there should be less potential for mixing assemblages and components. In any case, the number of items that fall into these uncertain provenience areas is small and does not alter the general interpretations and conclusions offered below.

CERAMIC ANALYSIS

Introduction

In recent years there has been an abundance of material published on American Bottom archaeology in conjunction with the FAI-270 project. Among other contributions, the sites investigated here have provided a wealth of data on pre-Mississippian and Mississippian ceramics and phases. From this research, Bareis and Porter (1984:-12) devised a new chronology for the American Bottom that refines the previous chronology established at the 1971 Cahokia Ceramic Conference (Fowler and Hall 1972). For this paper, the relevant changes in chronology occur in the Unnamed or Jarrot phase (A.D. 800-900) and Fairmount phase (A.D. 900-1050). The Unnamed or Jarrot phase has been abandoned in favor of the more clearly defined Loyd phase (A.D. 800-900) in the northern part of the American Bottom. The Fairmount phase was divided into the Merrell (A.D. 900-950) and Edelhardt (A.D. 950-1000) phases of the Emergent Mississippian period for the same geographic area (Kelly et al. 1984:128). The latest part of the Fairmount phase was considered to be fully Mississippian and is referred to as the Lohmann phase (A.D. 1000-1050) in the recent terminology. The temporal boundaries of the Stirling (A.D. 1050-1150), Moorehead (A.D. 1150-1250), and Sand Prairie (A.D. 1250-1400) phases using the new chronology are roughly the same as those of Fowler and Hall (1972), and the same phase names have been retained. However, some of the ceramic attributes and ceramic types associated with these phases have been amended. In addition, recent work in the American Bottom in conjunction with the FAI-270 project has greatly enhanced current knowledge of these later Mississippian Phases, including information on settlement sizes, community organization and patterning, mortuary behavior, and a greatly refined knowledge of the material assemblages (see Milner et al. 1984, Emerson and Jackson 1984, Phillips et al. 1980, Milner and Williams 1984, Milner 1983).

Due to the lack of specific provenience information and the probable mixed nature of large parts of the 1931 Powell Mound collection, it is difficult to assign the majority of the 1931 collections to any specific phase on any other basis than that of ceramic attributes. The recent highway-related work in the American Bottom noted above has provided a tremendous amount of data on changes in spatial organization, community plans, and architectural construction styles for some of the Emergent Mississippian and Mississippian occupations in the region. Unfortunately, the assemblage under consideration is analyzable only in terms of material culture and rough provenience data. In the following discussions, both the Fowler and Hall (1972) phases and more recently defined phases will be used. This is not done to confuse, but to underscore the problems involved in assigning phases to collections on the basis of material culture attributes alone. In addition, the FAI-270 chronology and phases were defined using materials that were not excavated from Cahokia proper. Since the Powell Mound collections are from Cahokia, they might differ somewhat from assemblages derived from the surrounding communities. The use of the Fairmount Phase as a temporal delineator may be justified since it was initially defined on the basis of collections from Cahokia proper rather than surrounding communities. When dealing with historical collections of limited spatial extent and vague vertical provenience, analysts may of necessity have to employ temporal units of less precision than is desired.

Analytical Procedures

Two objectives controlled the analytical procedures for the collections: (1) to provide a basic description of this unreported assemblage, and (2) to determine temporal variation between the premound, depression fill, and mound matrix activity episodes. Due to the lack of provenience data for the majority of sherds, a purely descriptive approach was viewed as a necessary first step in analysis. After the descriptive aspect was complete, rim sherds that could be assigned to one of these gross provenience locations were separated for more detailed attribute and chronological phase determination.

To accomplish the descriptive objective, it was decided to eschew any computer-oriented codification of the ceramics in favor of manual separation of the sherds according to attributes. By focusing initially on attributes rather than previously established ceramic types, some sherds not possessing specific type criteria would still be amenable to classification. Type names were applied after separation when applicable to specific attribute combinations. This approach has some methodological similarities to that used by Vogel (1975). Since different attributes were used in this analysis, specific attribute combinations derived here are not completely congruent with Vogel's categories.

Consisting of four variables, a hierarchical division of attributes was used for the pottery separation (Table 1). Two initial categories were delineated, rim sherds and body sherds, which were treated separately in the analysis. Table 2 associates the attribute combinations according to previously established types (see Griffin 1949; Griffin and Jones 1977; Gregg 1975; Vogel 1975; Fowler and Hall 1972, 1975). These classifications must be perceived as general approximations of ceramic types due to the variation present within the established types.

Body sherds

The body sherd classification shows a ceramic assemblage consisting of Bluff through Mississippian materials. Table 3 lists numerically the results of the body sherd classification according to temper, exterior/interior surface treatment, and decoration. As this table shows, shell-tempered ceramics predominate in the assemblage, and this finding must be viewed as a reflection of the general time period of active site utilization. Specific phases represented are predominantly Fairmount (or Emergent Mississippian), Stirling and Moorehead. Representation of phases will be discussed in greater detail through analysis of the rim sherds with provenience information.

Rim sherds

The rim sherd analysis (Tables 4 and 5) followed the same procedures used in the body sherd classification, with the addition of a vessel form variable based on rim and lip

Table 1. Variables and attributes used in the classification of ceramics from the Powell Mound. All attributes are applied uniformly to each sherd, creating a paradigmatic classification.

Variable 1. Location within vessel

- A) Rim
- B) Body
- C) Appendage

Variable 2. Temper

- A) Grit
- B) Grog
- C) Grit and grog
- D) Limestone (includes limestone and grog)
- E) Shell
- F) Shell and grog (includes grog tempered with shell)

Variable 3. Exterior/Interior surface treatment. Both surfaces are always examined, and listings in tables are always exterior first. Red-slipped includes all degrees of shading except for black and very dark grey.

- A) Plain (pl)
- B) Plain and polished (pl-pol)
- C) Red-slipped (rs)
- D) Red-slipped and polished (rs-pol)
- E) Black-slipped (bs)
- F) Black-slipped and polished (bs-pol)
- G) Cordmarked (cm)
- H) Cordmarked and smoothed (cm-sm)
- I) Cordmarked and red slipped (cm-rs)

Variable 4. Decoration

- A) None
- B) Incising (in)
- C) Punctation (pu)
- D) Incising and punctation (in-pu)
- E) Brushing
- F) Engraving
- G) Painting
- H) Painting and incising
- I) Notching

Table 2. Ceramic types and correlative attribute combinations used in this study.

PETERS STATION
- Grit cm/pl[1]
- Grit-grog cm/pl

KANE
- Grit cm/pl
- Grit-grog cm/pl
- Grog cm/pl; cm/bs; cm/rs

LOYD PLAIN
- Grit pl/pl (pink)
- Grit-grog pl/pl (pink)

LOYD CORDMARKED
- Grit cm/pl (pink)
- Grit-grog cm/pl (pink); cm/pl; cm/bs
- Grog cm/pl; cm/bs(?); cm/rs(?)

STUMPWARE
- Grit cm/pl (thick)
- Grit-grog cm/pl (thick)

MERRELL RED FILMED
- Grit rs/pl
- Grit-grog rs/pl; bs/pl; rs/rs
- Grog rs/pl; bs/pl; pl/rs; rs/rs; bs/rs; pl/bs; rs/bs; bs/bs; bs-pol/rs
- Limestone-grog rs/pl; bs/pl

MONKS MOUND RED
- Limestone rs/pl; rs-pu/pl; rs/rs; bs/rs; rs-pol/rs; rs-pu/rs; rs/bs

MONKS MOUND PLAIN
- Limestone pl/pl; pl/bs; pl-pol/pl; bs-pol/bs
- Limestone-grog rs-pol/pl

PULCHER PLAIN
- Limestone pl-pol/pl; bs-pol/bs
- Limestone-grog rs-pol/pl

PULCHER CORDMARKED
- Limestone cm/pl; cm/rs; cm/bs; sm-cm/pl
- Limestone-grog cm/pl; cm/rs; sm-cm/pl

PULCHER RED FILMED
- Limestone-grog rs/bs

CAHOKIA RED FILMED
- Shell rs-pol/pl-in; rs/pl-pu; rs/rs; rs-pol/rs; rs-pol/rs-lu; rs/rs-pu; rs/rs-holes; pl/bs
- Shell-grog rs/pl; bs/pl; rs/rs; bs/rs; rs/bs; bs/bs

POWELL PLAIN
- Shell rs-pl/ rs-pol/pl; bs/pl; bs-pol/pl; rs/rs; rs-pol/rs; bs-pol/rs; bs/bs; bs-pol/bs
- Shell-grog rs-pol/pl; bs-pol/pl; rs-pol/rs; bs-pol/bs

RAMEY INCISED
- Shell bs-pol-in/pl
- Shell-grog bs-pol-in/pl

ST. CLAIR PLAIN
- Shell pl/pl; pl-pol/pl; rs(lip only)/pl; bs(lip only)/pl; pl/rs/; pl/bs
- Shell-grog pl/pl; pl-pol/pl; pl/rs; pl/bs

CAHOKIA CORDMARKED
- Shell cm/pl; cm-rs/pl; brushed/pl; cm/rs; cm-rs/rs
- Shell-grog cm/pl; cm/rs; cm-rs/rs

[1]The following abbreviations are used: Surface treatments--rs=red-slipped; bs=black-slipped; pol=polished; pl=plain; cm=cordmarked; sm=smoothed; xxx/xxx indicates exterior/interior surface treatment. Decorations--pu=punctations; in=incising; lu=lugs. Temper types are listed first.

Table 3. Body sherds from Powell Mound arranged by temper and surface treatment attributes. All proveniences are combined.

SURFACE TREATMENT	TEMPER						
	Grit	Grog	Grit-Grog	Lime-Stone	Shell	Shell-Grog	Total
pl/pl[1]	1	53	9	8	730	42	843
pl-pol/pl		4		6	40	9	159
pl/rs	1	7		2	543	40	593
pl/bs		3		2	79	6	90
cm/pl	10	22	15	13	16	3	79
cm/rs		17		2	9	3	31
cm/bs		2	1	1			4
cm-sm/pl		1		2			3
cm-rs/pl					4		4
cm-rs/rs					3	1	4
rs/pl		8	4	28	470	25	535
rs/rs	1	9	1	48	240	27	326
rs/bs		4		2	11	5	22
rs-pol/pl				9	72	9	90
rs-pol/rs				11		5	16
bs/pl		3	3	2	46	5	59
bs/rs		36		2	48	3	89
bs/bs		5			18	2	25
bs-pol/pl					72	2	74
bs-pol/rs		2			6	3	11
bs-pol/bs				2	13	1	16
Stumpware		1					1
Decorated		2		5	50	3	60
Unknown			1	4	144	5	154
TOTAL	13	179	34	149	2714	199	3288

[1]The following abbreviations are used: Surface treatments--rs = red-slipped; bs = black-slipped; pol = polished; pl = plain; cm = cordmarked; sm = smoothed; xxx/xxx indicates exterior/interior surface treatment.

Table 4. Rim sherds from Powell Mound arranged by surface treatment and temper.

SURFACE TREATMENT	TEMPER						
	Grit	Grog	Grit-Grog	Lime-Stone	Shell	Shell-Grog	Total
pl/pl[1]			1		16		17
pl/pl (pink)			3				3
pl-pol/pl		1			5		6
pl-pol/rs		2					2
pl/rs					86	4	90
pl/rs					5	1	6
pl/bs					3		3
cm/pl			2	3			5
cm-sm/pl		1					1
cm-sm-rs/pl				1			1
rs/pl					12		12
rs/pl					5		5
rs(lip)/pl					11		11
rs/rs		2		11	59	4	76
rs/rs				1	6		7
rs-pol/pl				2	4		6
rs-pol/pl						1	1
rs-pol/rs		1			9	3	12
rs-pol/rs					3		3
bs(lip)/pl					5		5
bs/rs		1			5	1	7
bs/bs					6		6
bs-pol/pl					6	3	7
bs-pol/pl					2		2
bs-pol/rs				1			1
bs-pol/bs				2	12		13
White slip					1		1
bs-pol/bs						1	1
Stumpware			1				1
Unknown				1	19	1	21
TOTAL	0	8	7	22	280	19	336

[1]The following abbreviations are used: Surface treatments--rs = red-slipped; bs = black-slipped; pol = polished; pl = plain; cm = cordmarked; sm = smoothed; xxx/xxx indicates exterior/interior surface treatment.

Table 5. Rim sherds from Powell Mound, segregated by temper and vessel form attributes.

VESSEL AND RIM FORM	TEMPER						
	Grit	Grog	Grit-Grog	Lime-Stone	Shell	Shell-Grog	Total
JAR							
Vertical		5	4	3	15	3	30
Pre-Powell					36		36
Powell flared					47		47
Powell rolled					20		20
Flared		1			41	5	47
Extended rim						2	2
JUICE JAR							
Vertical					11		11
BOWL							
Vertical			3	13	49	2	66
Flared				1	7		8
Constricted				3	20	1	24
PLATE					3		3
SALT PAN		1			1		4
BEAKER					1	1	2
WATER BOTTLE				1	2		3
OTHER		1			6		7
UNKNOWN				1	13	5	19
TOTAL	0	8	7	22	280	19	336

shape. Again, shell-tempered ceramics dominate the assemblage, with jar and bowl forms associated with the late Fairmount (Lohmann phase in the FAI-270 chronology) to Stirling phase most common. Cahokia Red-filmed, Powell Plain, and Ramey Incised types were most commonly represented in the rim sherds, based on the attribute combinations seen in Tables 4 and 5.

Rim sherds that could be assigned to one of the three gross provenience categories described above were pulled from the general collections and grouped by spatial context. Type names were determined for each of these provenienced rim sherds, with the type names and phases included for each vessel represented. Figures 6, 7, and 8 show selected rim profiles from these major provenience areas. Additional drawings of rim profiles are stored with the collections at the Illinois State Museum.

A closer examination of the rims with provenience indicates that the premound provenience is represented by a predominance of Fairmount phase (FAI-270 Lohmann phase) ceramics (Table 6, Figure 6). The ceramic types associated with these phases are a Jarrot-phase pink-fired jar (also known as Madison Shale ware) with a paste common to the Emergent Mississippian period in the American Bottom and adjacent uplands, Cahokia Red-filmed, Monks Mound Red, and some early forms of Powell Plain jars. The flared-rim, smoothed-over, cordmarked jar (Figure 6i) is an anomalous vessel for the Cahokia site. The cordmarking, rather than being vertical, is parallel to the rim, and this is an uncommon trait in this area for vessels of this time period. The vessel form and rim shape correspond more closely to Baytown series ceramics (Phillips 1970). This may represent a vessel that was manufactured in the

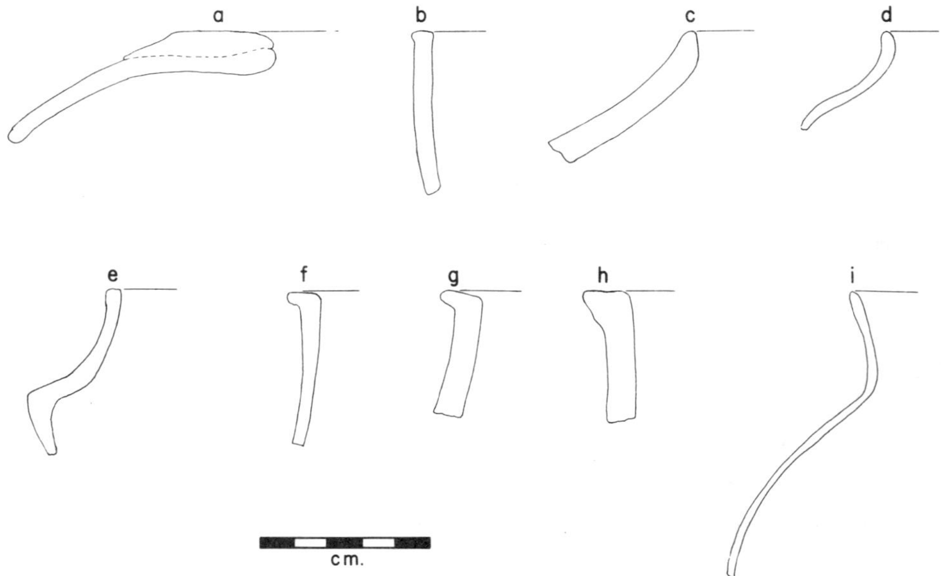

Figure 6. Rim profiles for selected sherds from premound proveniences: (a) constricted-mouth bowl, rs/pl; (b) vertical-rim Monks Mound Red bowl, rs/rs; (c) vertical short-necked jar, rs/rs-lip only; (d) vertical short-necked jar with rolled rim, bs/pl-pol; (e) vertical rim jar with "hyperangular" shoulder common to Lohmann phase, pl/pl; (f) vertical-rim Powell Plain jar, bs-pol/bs; (g) vertical rim Cahokia Red-filmed jar, pl/rs; (h) thickened vertical rim St. Clair Plain jar, pl/pl; (i) flared-rim, grog-tempered jar with horizontal cordmarking, sm-cm/pl. Keys to abbreviations provided in Tables 1-8.

Table 6. Vessel forms, ceramic types and associated phases for rim sherds from premound proveniences.

CERAMIC TYPE	SURFACE TREATMENT	VESSEL FORM	RIM FORM	NUMBER
JARROT OR UNNAMED PHASE (FAI-270 LOYD PHASE)				
Madison Shale	pl/pl[1](pink)	Jar	Vertical	1
JARROT TO FAIRMOUNT PHASE (FAI-270 LOYD TO LOHMANN PHASES)				
Cahokia Red-filmed	rs/rs	Jar	Vertical	1
FAIRMOUNT (?) PHASE				
Powell Plain	pl-pol/pl	Jar	Vertical	1
	pol	Bowl(?)	Handle	2
Stumpware	cm/pl	Unknown	Vertical	1
FAIRMOUNT PHASE (FAI-270 MERRELL TO LOHMANN PHASES)				
Monks Mound Red	rs-pol/rs	Bowl	Vertical	1
	rs-no-brushed/rs	Jar	Flared	1
Cahokia Red-filmed	rs/rs	Bowl	Constricted	2
Powell Plain	pl/pl	Jar	Flared	1
	rs/rs	Jar	Pre-Powell	1
		Jar	Flared	2
	bs-pol/bs	Jar	Pre-Powell	2
		Bowl	Vertical	1
STIRLING PHASE				
St. Clair Plain	rs(lip only)/pl	Jar	Rolled	1
UNKNOWN PHASE				
Unknown	rs-pol/rs	Jar	Flared	1
	cm-sm/pl	Jar	Flared	1
	-----	Pipe(?)	-----	1
			TOTAL	21

[1]The following abbreviations are used: Surface treatments--rs = red-slipped; bs = black-slipped; pol = polished; pl = plain; cm = cordmarked; sm = smoothed; xxx/xxx indicates exterior/interior surface treatment. Decorations--no = notched.

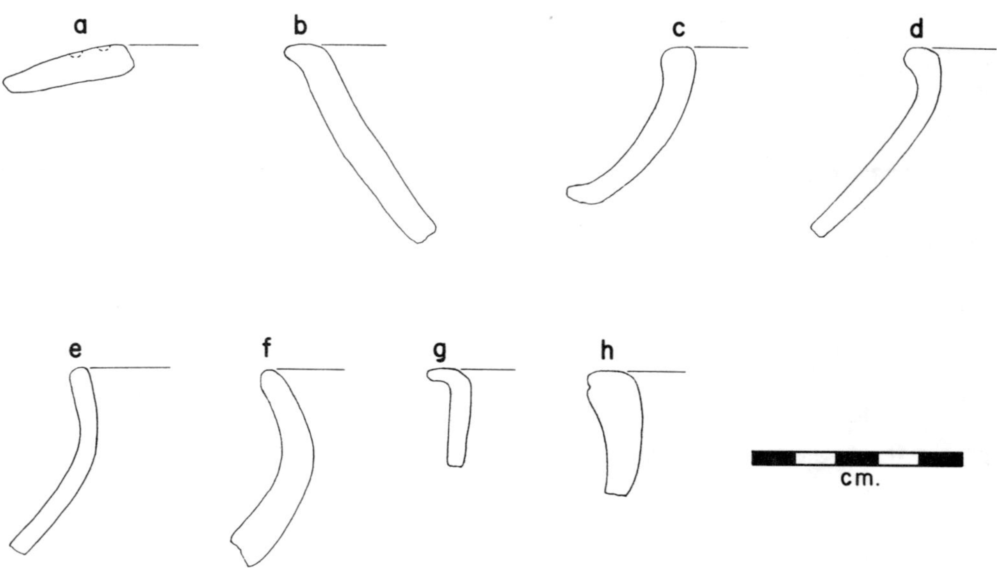

Figure 7. Rim profiles for selected sherds from depression fill proveniences: (a) constricted-mouth bowl with two rows of punctations, rs-pu/pl; (b) Cahokia Red-filmed bowl, pl/rs; (c) vertical-rim Cahokia Red-filmed jar with fugitive red slip, rs/rs; (d) vertical-rim, short-necked Powell Plain jar, bs-pol/pl; (e) slightly flared-rim Cahokia Red-filmed jar, rs/rs (exterior slip fugitive); (f) flared-rim Cahokia Red-filmed jar, rs/rs; (g) extruded-rim Cahokia Red-filmed jar, rs/rs; (h) vertical thickened-rim Cahokia Red-filmed jar, pl/rs. Keys to abbreviations provided in Tables 1-8.

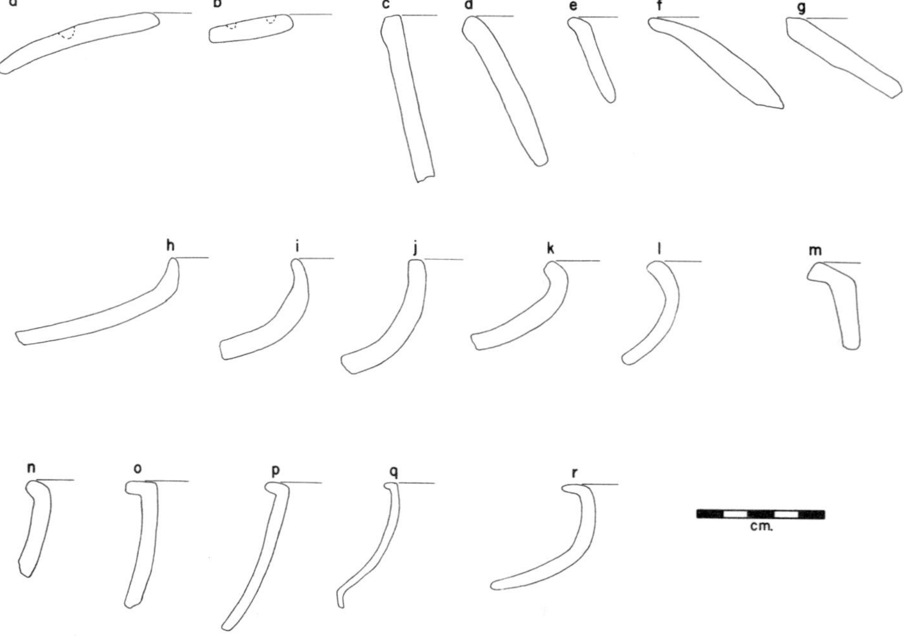

Figure 8. Rim profiles for selected sherds from mound matrix proveniences: (a, b) Constricted-mouth punctated bowl, rs-pu/pl; (c, d) Cahokia Red-filmed bowl, pl/rs; (e) Monks Mound Red bowl, rs/rs; (f, g) Cahokia Red-filmed shallow bowl, pl/rs; (h) Merrell Cordmarked short-necked jar with vertical exterior cord impressions, sm-cm/pl-pol; (i) slightly flared Cahokia Red-filmed jar, pl/rs; (j) vertical-rim St. Clair Plain jar, pl/pl; (k) vertical rolled-rim short-necked jar with notched lip and vertical brushing on exterior, pl-brushed/rs; (l) flared-rim Cahokia Red-filmed jar, pl/rs; (m) Cahokia Red-filmed flared-rim bowl, pl/rs (lip only); (n) vertical rolled-rim Cahokia Red-filmed jar, pl/rs; (o) extruded-rim Powell Plain jar, pol-rs (lip only)/pl; (p) extruded-rim Powell Plain jar, bs-pol/pl; (q) rolled-rim Powell Plain jar, bs-pol/bs-pol; (r) extruded-rim Cahokia Red-filmed jar, pl/rs. Keys to abbreviations provided in Tables 1-8.

lower Mississippi Valley. It was recovered from an intrusive pit that may have disturbed earlier deposits in the general premound occupation.

The depression fill ceramics (Table 7, Figure 7) represent a somewhat later but overlapping series of ceramic types and associated phases. The Fairmount phase (FAI-270 Lohmann phase) is represented by a number of Cahokia Red-filmed jars with vertical rims. Stirling and possibly Moorehead phases are also associated with the Cahokia Red-filmed type, but the latter phase displays a greater proportion of everted and flared rim shapes than are present in this sample. Most of the depression fill can probably be assigned to the Stirling phase.

The mound matrix provenience unit displays the greatest variety in ceramic types and associated phases (Table 8, Figure 8). Emergent Mississippian and Lohmann phases (or Fairmount phase ceramics) are evidenced by vertical-rimmed jars and early Powell Plain rim forms with rolled and short, flared rims. The later Stirling (or possibly Moorehead) phases are exhibited in the Cahokia Red-filmed and St. Clair Plain sherds. The majority of the rims would easily fall into the Stirling phase, and the majority of the early construction activities at the Powell Mound most probably date to that phase.

Our interpretations of the variety of phases and ceramic types from the mound

Table 7. Vessel forms, ceramic types and associated phases for rim sherds from depression fill proveniences.

CERAMIC TYPE	SURFACE TREATMENT	VESSEL FORM	RIM FORM	NUMBER
FAIRMOUNT PHASE (PRIMARILY FAI-270 LOHMANN PHASE)				
Cahokia Red-filmed	rs/rs	Jar	Vertical	1
		Jar	Flared	1
	pl/rs	Bowl	Vertical	1
STIRLING PHASE				
Cahokia Red-filmed	rs/rs	Jar	Rolled	1
	rs/pl-pu	Bowl	Constricted	1
Powell Plain	pl/bs	Jar	?	1
	rs-pol/rs	Jar	Everted	1
St.Clair Plain	rs(lip only)/pl	Bowl	Flared	1
STIRLING TO MOOREHEAD PHASES				
Cahokia Red-filmed	pl/rs	Jar	Flared	1
	rs/rs	Jar	Flared	2
Unknown type	pl/rs	Plate	-----	1
			TOTAL	12

[1]The following abbreviations are used: Surface treatments--rs = red slipped; bs = black slipped; pol = polished; pl = plain; xxx/xxx indicates exterior/interior surface treatment. Decorations--pu = punctations. Keys to abbreviations provided in Tables 1-8.

Table 8. Ceramic types, vessel forms and associated phases for rim sherds from mound matrix proveniences.

CERAMIC TYPE	SURFACE TREATMENT	VESSEL FORM	RIM FORM	NUMBER
JARROT PHASE (FAI-270 LOYD PHASE)				
Pulcher Cordmarked	cm-sm-rs/pl[1]	Jar	Vertical	1
JARROT TO FAIRMOUNT PHASE (FAI-270 LOYD TO LOHMANN PHASES)				
Cahokia Red-filmed	pl/rs	Jar	Vertical	1
FAIRMOUNT PHASE (FAI-270 MERRELL TO LOHMANN PHASES, PRIMARILY LOHMANN)				
Monks Mound Red	rs/rs	Bowl	Vertical	1
		Bowl	Flared	1
Powell Plain	rs/rs	Jar	Pre-Powell	1
		Jar	Flared	1
	rs-pol/pl	Jar	Flared	1
	bs/bs	Jar	Pre-Powell	1
	bs-pol/pl	Jar	Flared	1
	bs-pol/rs	Jar	Pre-Powell	1
	bs-pol/bs	Jar	Pre-Powell	1
Cahokia Red-filmed	rs/pl	Jar	Pre-Powell	1
	rs/rs	Jar	Flared	1
	pl/rs	Bowl	Vertical	3
	rs/pl	Bowl	Constricted	1
	rs/pl-pu	Bowl	Constricted	1
	rs/pl-in	Bowl	Constricted	1
	rs/rs-pu	Bowl	Constricted	1
	rs/rs-in	Bowl	Constricted	1
	rs/rs holes	Bowl	Constricted	1
STIRLING PHASE				
Powell Plain	pl/rs	Jar	Rolled	1
Cahokia Red-filmed	rs/pl-pu	Bowl	Constricted	1
STIRLING TO MOOREHEAD PHASES				
Cahokia Red-filmed	pl/rs	Jar	Flared	3
	pl/bs	Jar	Flared	1
Unknown type	pl/rs	Plate	-----	2
MOOREHEAD PHASE				
Cahokia Red-filmed	rs/rs	Bowl	Vertical	4
MOOREHEAD TO SAND PRAIRIE PHASES				
Cahokia Red-filmed	rs/rs	Jar	Flared	3
St. Clair Plain	pl/pl	Bowl	Vertical	1
	rs/rs	Bowl	Flared	1
	rs(lip only)/pl	Bowl	Flared	1
UNKNOWN PHASE				
Unknown type	polished	Beaker	Handle	1
Unknown type	in-no-brushed/rs	Jar	Flared	2
			TOTAL	43

[1]The following abbreviations are used: Surface treatments--rs = red-slipped; bs = black-slipped; pol = polished; pl = plain; cm = cordmarked; sm = smoothed; xxx/xxx indicates exterior/interior surface treatment. Decorations--pu = punctations; in = incising; lu = lugs; no = notched.

matrix do not suggest that mound construction was continuous from the Jarrot or Emergent Mississippian through Moorehead phases. Rather, the predominance of ceramics from the Stirling phase indicates a later time period for the majority of mound construction activities. Construction of even the small core areas in the Powell Mound required large volumes of sediment from the surrounding area. As noted earlier, the dark color of the lower portion of the Powell Mound fill indicates that much of the volume of the first construction stages was derived from topsoils; these sediments would likely contain cultural materials from earlier phases. The mound construction activities would have to date to the later time periods represented in the mound matrix.

The distribution of ceramics does not indicate that there is a clear separation between the premound, depression fill, and mound matrix components. There appears to be relatively continuous occupation and activity in the Powell Mound area throughout these episodes. This continuum of occupation and mound construction activities seems to correspond to the florescence of other mound construction activities seen in the American Bottom (Fowler and Hall 1975, Porter 1974, Fowler n.d.). The early Mississippian Stirling phase is closely associated with increased mound construction as indicated in the Powell Mound assemblage by the mound matrix component.

Discussion

It can be seen from the above statements that our interpretations regarding the contemporaneity of the premound and mound matrix materials also differs from interpretations offered by Kelley (1933) and Kelley and Cole (1931). Those authors discuss the similarity of materials from the premound and mound components, but the interpretations were based on gross inspection of the ceramics and not on formal analyses. It should also be noted that based on what was known of Cahokia ceramic chronology in 1931, their conclusions were entirely supportable. More stratigraphically controlled assemblages are available for comparison now, and the Cahokia ceramic chronology is understandably more refined. The examination of the rim sherds with provenience does indicate a large amount of phase overlap between the three provenience components, but this overlap is consistent with continuity of activities in the Powell Mound area. The lack of complete overlap of components suggests continuous occupation instead of contemporaneity. However, the total span of time represented in the assemblage at hand is probably short and may be limited to the later Fairmount (i.e. Lohmann) and early Stirling phases.

The land utilization of the Powell Mound area changed in concert with the general evolution of the Cahokia site. The premound component at the Powell Mound reflects a more or less generalized habitation or village area that is not directly involved with mound construction activities. As part of the lithic assemblage indicates, though, the later part of the premound occupation may have involved specialized features that are more directly related to the beginnings of mound construction and specialized nondomicilliary activities in the Powell Mound area. Later site utilization during the Stirling and Moorehead phases is clearly associated with major mound construction activities in the Powell Mound area as well as in other parts of the Cahokia site.

The Powell Mound ceramic assemblage contains a few foreign sherds indicating some degree of connection with other contemporaneous Mississippian communities. One sherd tentatively identified as Holly Fine Engraved, probably from the Caddo area, is present in the mound matrix component. Possible affiliation with the lower Mississippi Valley is suggested by the presence of a grog-tempered and smoothed-over cordmarked Baytown series vessel. Other nonlocal associations are indicated by the presence of a Nodena White-filmed rim and a red-and-white painted body sherd (Phillips 1970). Nodena phase materials originate in the lower Mississippi River valley. Both of these are from general unprovenienced trench excavations but are most likely associated with the mound matrix provenience and the later activity episodes in particular. Because of the lack of contextual data, it is not possible to address the processes by which these sherds accumulated in the Powell Mound assemblage. Their presence does suggest that external interaction with other Mississippian cultural groups occurred during the Stirling and Moorehead phases.

In summation, the premound component at the Powell Mound seems to be associated mainly with the early Fairmount phase or Lohmann phase of the FAI-270 chronology. The depression fill and mound matrix components are temporally close, with a preponderance of Stirling phase ceramics in the Mound matrix. Flared-rim bowls and jars are present in these later components but are not present in the premound component. Mound construction activities apparently extend into the Moorehead phase; the last major construction stage of the Powell Mound may be associated with this phase. No unequivocal evidence of Sand Prairie phase ceramics was recovered from the mound matrix component.

LITHICS

Chipped stone

Many collections from Cahokia and other Mississippian sites do not contain numerous formal chipped-stone tools. In many cases, even debitage is less numerous than in earlier cultural systems. Upon preliminary inspection of the Powell Mound collections, it appeared that this assemblage was more prolific in lithic items than usual for late prehistoric sites. Hundreds of debitage flakes as well as occasional projectile points and utilized flakes were present. Later and more detailed inspection of the lithics, their formal qualities, and their proveniences contradicted this initial impression of a generalized and abundant lithic assemblage. Even the premound Emergent Mississippian assemblages did not display a wide range of formal tools and reduction debitage.

The formal attributes of the chipped-stone items indicated that the majority were associated with the production trajectory of a particular tool type. A generalized utilitarian tool assemblage was not indicated. Instead, the assemblage apparently represents the complete production trajectory for prismatic microdrills. All stages of this trajectory are apparently present, from initial core preparation and maintenance to actual microdrill production and replacement of exhausted tools. To deal with this specialized manufacturing sequence, the lithic sorting was designed to explicate the stages in this trajectory. Preliminary sorting was performed and categories were established based on descriptive morphological attributes. Detailed use-wear analyses were not performed for the entire assemblage due to time constraints.

Eight major morphological categories were used in the initial sorting (Figure 9). Amorphous cores take the form of large angular chert blocks that show unsystematic flake removal scars in several surface planes (Figure 9a). A microdrill core is any item, regardless of its other formal attributes, that shows flake removal scars characteristic of microdrill blank production. This process is accomplished by longitudinal removal of flakes from acute-angled margins. The scars are long and narrow, reminiscent of blade production, and are usually coincident with core margins (Figures 9b and 9c). Flakes are thin items with striking platform remnants and/or a definable bulb of percussion. No attempt was made to segregate different types

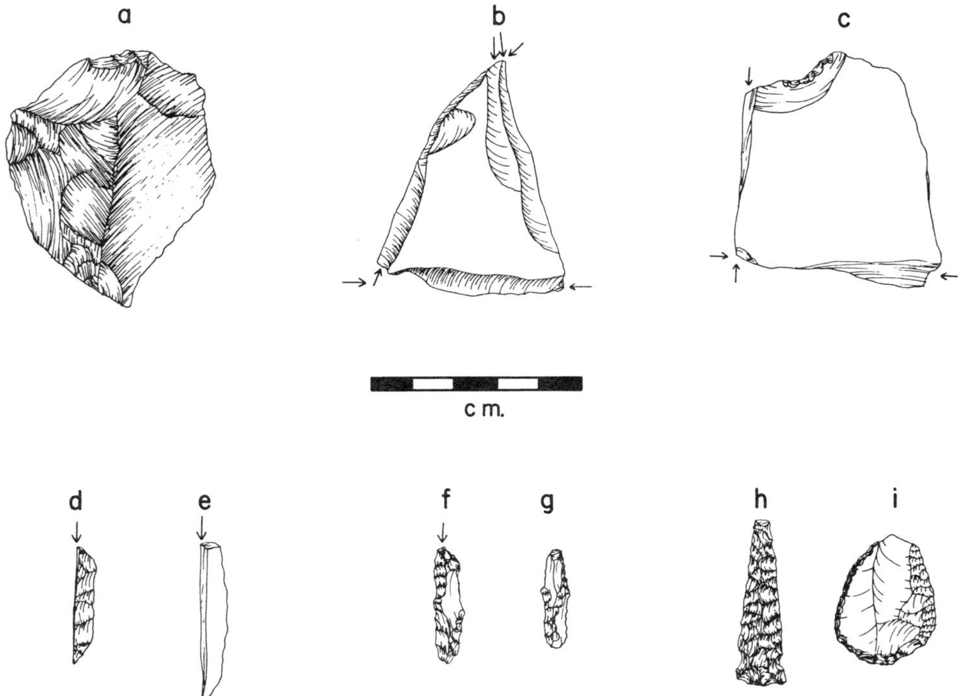

Figure 9. Chipped-stone categories for the Powell Mound lithic assemblage; arrows indicate directions of force for microdrill spall removals: (a) amorphous core from pit in 100R12; (b, c) microdrill cores from pit in 100L1; (d) unused microdrill spall from unit 130R1; (e) unused microdrill spall from pit in 100 L1; (f, g) used microdrills from pit in 100 R16; (h) Madison side-notched projectile point, no provenience; (i) shaped end scraper, no provenience.

of flakes based on the presence of cortex or evidence of prior flake removals. Shatter or chert chunks are irregular angular items that lack core or flake attributes. These are unclassifiable lithic debitage items that may come from any stage of manufacturing or any type of manufacturing trajectory. Prismatic spall is the term used here to decribe the narrow flakes removed from the microdrill cores (Figures 9d and 9e). These are long and narrow, similar to blades in width to length ratio, and generally have a triangular or quadrilateral cross-section. Microdrills (Figures 9f and 9g) are prismatic spalls with use-wear attrition on the lateral and distal margins in the form of rounding and/or crushing. These six categories represent a specialized manufacturing trajectory oriented toward the production and utilization of the microdrills. This collection compares favorably with the microdrill assemblage described by Mason and Perino (1961) from a tract near the Kunneman Mound group at the northern end of the Cahokia site.

Two additional chipped-stone categories were recognized that are part of this production sequence. Hoe chips exhibit characteristic use polish and striations resulting from repeated contact with materials with high silica content. Bifaces include all intentionally retouched bifacial implements, including projectile points (Figure 9h), knives, preforms, and fragments. The shaped end scraper shown in Figure 9i is unique in the assemblage but has no definite provenience.

The raw materials represented in the Powell Mound collections are very uniform. About 98% of the chert items are made from locally derived Burlington chert, available in several localities on either side of the Mis-

Table 9. Distribution of chipped- and ground-stone categories by gross provenience units.

DESCRIPTIVE CATEGORY	PROVENIENCE							
	Premound	Mound Matrix	Fill	100L1 (Pit)	100R8 (Pit)	100R16 (Pit)	Unknown	Total
Chipped Stone								
Amorphous core			2		1	1	5	9
Microdrill core	1		9		6	3	29	48
Flake	3		176	1	6	4	72	262
Shatter			25	4	1	6	40	76
Prismatic spall	1		28		5	1	4	49
Microdrill	7		25		9		3	44
Hoe chip							1	1
Biface	1	1	1				2	5
Total	13	1	266	5	28	15	136	494
Ground Stone								
Hammerstone							4	4
Celts		1	1				2	4
"Palettes"				1	1		3	5
Grooved abraders	2	2	1				7	12
Edge abraders			3	5		6	20	34
Total	2	3	5	6	1	6	36	59

sissippi River near Cahokia. Much of this material compared favorably to chert from the Crescent Hills locality, described by Ives (1975). Since it is not known if these items actually came from the Crescent Hills quarries, the more conservative and general designation as Burlington formation chert will be used here. All Burlington material in the collections appears to be high-grade micro- to crypto-crystalline chert with few visible fossil inclusions. Heat treatment of the items was not readily observable either in the form of discoloration or changes in surface luster. The remainder of the collection is composed of Mill Creek chert (the single hoe chip) and two distinct but unidentified chert types. All of the material associated with the proposed microdrill manufacturing trajectory is Burlington chert.

Table 9 summarizes the distribution of these items by descriptive category in the Powell Mound collections. The majority of the lithic items are associated with the premound pit features, specifically pits in unit 100L1 and 100R16. These provenience units also exhibit the entire microdrill production sequence, whereas other provenience units do not. This would suggest that these premound pits are directly associated with production of the microdrills. This conclusion is further supported when patterns of utilization are considered. Presence of use-wear attrition on flake and shatter categories is generally restricted to nonpit proveniences. Only two nonmicrodrill items from pit proveniences show visible use-wear attrition. This pattern holds even though numerous flake and shatter items are present in the pits, and these are of a quality and size sufficient for modification into a variety of flake tool forms or for immediate use. The flakes in the pits are interpreted as by-products of the specialized microdrill manufacturing sequence that were not considered for use in other contexts. The pit in 100R8 shows the entire microdrill production and disposal sequence. These items were evidently not only produced but also disposed of as a group, associated with a specific and restricted set of activities. Recent excavations at several sites with Lohmann phase components demonstrate that microdrill production and use are not restricted to specific mound contexts and are most often associated with this earliest Mississippian phase in the region (Milner et al. 1984).

The function of these microdrills has been debated for years. Mason and Perino (1961) and Perino (1971) report finding numerous microdrills in a tract near the Kunneman Mound group north of Monks Mound. Vander Leest (1980:254) reported a localized concentration of microdrill cores, prismatic spalls, and utilized microdrills from the surface of a small area of the southern Dunham Tract (between Powell Mound and Monks Mound). Although these items are morphologically similar to the Powell Mound artifacts, they are not found in direct association with any potentially worked raw materials.

It has been proposed that these items were used in the manufacture of perforated shell beads, but it was not until recently that this idea was tested at least in a preliminary fashion. Lawrence Keeley (Newcomer and Keeley 1979, Keeley 1980, Van Noten, Cahen and Keeley 1980) worked extensively with high-magnification microscopic identification of use-wear polishes and reported a high rate of success in determining the type of raw material on which specific tools were used. In 1980, Keeley examined two of the microdrills from the Powell Mound collections and reported that the polish present compared favorably with polish derived from experimental shell working. Neither of the archaeological specimens compared favorably with experimental polish resulting from working hide, bone, wood, or meat. In addition, inspection by Ahler of the microflake attrition patterns and edge modifications using low-magnification techniques indicated that the items were used as rotary perforators. Both the microscopic and macroscopic attributes strongly suggested that these items were both formally and functionally unifacial perforators. Recently, Yerkes (1983) obtained the utilized microdrills from the Powell Mound and performed a more detailed and experimentally controlled high-magnification analysis of these items. His conclusions confirmed the initial observations of Keeley, providing strong evidence that these items were used for shell perforation.

Unfortunately, few shell items were recovered from the same Powell Mound proveniences as the microdrill assemblage. None of the shell items that were associated with the microdrills show evidence of extensive perforation or modification. This finding indicates that the use of the microdrills may have taken place at activity areas remote from the production and disposal loci. Studies by Keeley (Van Noten, Cahen, and Keeley 1980) indicated that whereas manufacture and disposal of items may take place in the same spatial locality, actual utilization of the products may be performed at activity areas spatially segregated from the production locality. In the case of the Powell Mound microdrill assemblage, there is strong evidence of production, use, and discard of exhausted microdrills in the pits beneath the initial core mounds. The lack of perforated and modified shell in these same loci could indicate that all modified shell items were removed from the manufacturing locus for use in specific contexts remote from the Powell Mound. Manufacture of perforated shell items may have taken place at the Powell Mound, but the final products were removed for use in other areas.

The context of disposal of the microdrill assemblage at Powell Mound is also of interest. Comparisons can be made to another large special-function lithic assemblage from Cahokia, the projectile point caches from

Mound 72 (Fowler and Hall 1975, Ahler 1977). One of three caches was found in a submound pit underneath the northwestern primary mound. The pit in the Powell Mound in unit 100L1 is directly underneath one of the core mounds noted by Deuel. These core mounds are interpreted here as initial primary mounds comparable to those observed in the excavation of Mound 72 (see Figure 5). Evidence from the ceramic assemblage indicates that the premound pits at Powell Mound are more closely associated with the mound matrix assemblage than with the remainder of the premound ceramics. This finding suggests that the microdrill assemblages in the premound pits may be associated with the actual mound construction sequence as initial offerings, caches, or special-purpose nonutilitarian items. Comparison of the ceramic assemblages of Mound 72 and the premound Powell Mound proveniences also indicates approximate contemporaneity of the assemblages. Both appear to date to the late Fairmount to early Stirling phases. Recent work by the University of Illinois on the FAI-270 Project in the American Bottom suggested that microdrill production and use in the Cahokia area was most prevalent during the Lohmann phase (Milner et al. 1984:165). The Lohmann phase is temporally equivalent to the late Fairmount phase in the chronological framework used here.

In contrast to the Mound 72 projectile point caches, the full manufacturing sequence appears to be present in the Powell Mound. At Mound 72, over 1,000 projectile points were found in three separate caches, but little evidence for the manufacture of these items was recovered; they were probably made elsewhere, possibly in areas remote from Cahokia. The Powell Mound assemblage shows the complement of this disposal of finished items; the manufacturing locus is known but the location of use and discard of the finished target product, the modified shell, remains unknown at this time.

It appears that Mound 72 and Powell Mound share some temporal and functional characteristics. Both involve specialized manufacture and/or disposal of special-function tools in restricted and nonutilitarian archaeological contexts. Both areas also involve initial primary mound construction activities that were later incorporated into large mound structures. Both areas are temporally associated with the Fairmount phase or possibly the more temporally restricted Lohmann phase. The nature of the manufacturing and disposal of the specialized items in both mounds indicates that these tools were utilized in activities involving larger segments of the Cahokia population than a single household or nuclear family. Neither context indicates that the items are the result of idiosyncratic behavior. Integrative sociopolitical activities involving large numbers of people and possibly several segments of the Cahokia community are indicated.

Tempering these temporal and depositional parallels between Mound 72 and Powell Mound is the fact that the Mound 72 projectile point caches are the final targeted products of the specialized manufacturing activities whereas the microdrills are only secondary production tools, used to shape the final targeted product, the modified shell items. Although the Powell Mound assemblages offer an opportunity to examine a task-specific manufacturing sequence, the artifacts recovered do not convey the same social implications as the projectile point caches from Mound 72.

Ground Stone

Five descriptive categories of ground stone items are recognized here with their respective proveniences (Table 9). Most numerous are edge abraders, which are thin fragments of sandstone with evidence of grinding, smoothing, and/or beveling on one or more lateral margins. These were referred to as "saws" in the original field notes. There is some tendency for these to be associated with the premound pits, and this pattern suggests that these abraders may be functionally associated with the microdrill assemblage. Perhaps they were used in the initial stages of shell modification. In the absence of detailed experimental replicative data for ground-stone items, it is not possible to test this suggestion using high-magnification inspection.

Summary

The lithic assemblage from the 1931 Powell Mound collections exhibits two major aspects. First and most unusual is the evidence of flaked-stone microdrill manufacturing and discard in the premound pits. Possibly associated with the flaked stone items are flat sandstone abraders with lateral edge modification. The microdrills were apparently used in the rotary perforation of shell items, based on a combination of low-magnification observation of edge attrition and use-wear flakes coupled with high-magnification observations of the use polish on the microdrills and comparison with experimental specimens. The general context of disposal of the microdrill assemblage may relate to other premound caches such as the projectile points under Mound 72.

The second observation is that the remainder of the lithic assemblage, that part not relatable to the microdrill trajectory, is very similar to other general lithic collections from Cahokia and other Middle Mississippian sites. Few formal tools are present, and emphasis is apparently placed on flake manufacture and utilization. Almost exclusively, locally available raw materials are used. Most of the latter aspect of the assemblage is from general mound or depression fill areas and probably represents general village habitation debris instead of specialized manufacturing activities. Inclusion of these items in the mound and depression fill probably resulted from the use of midden and secondary refuse in topsoil as borrowed fill for mound construction.

FAUNAL AND BOTANICAL REMAINS

Faunal remains from these collections exhibit moderately good preservation. The following description is only preliminary, since adequate provenience information is lacking for most of the items.

Human Remains

Included in the miscellaneous debris and the gross provenience bags are several specimens of human bone. Table 10 lists the identified human remains by known general provenience unit. All human remains apparently represent adults, and at least three individuals are present. No contextual information is available to indicate whether these remains represent intentional interments, are accidental inclusions in the mound fill, or are associated with construction and dedication of specific mound episodes, as are many of the burials in Mound 72. Indicative of possible ceremonial function of some of the human remains is a single, cut parietal fragment. Again, the context of this item is not clear, so little can be said concerning its significance.

Nonhuman Remains

The unmodified nonhuman faunal remains are listed in Table 11 by taxon and provenience. Many items may be identifiable to more precise taxonomic units than are indicated here. Since no screening was performed during excavation, it is not possible to offer reliable subsistence-oriented interpretations of the faunal remains. The only conclusions offered are that while there are numerous species and habitats represented, the majority of the identifiable remains are deer. Numerous worked bone and shell items were also identified in the collections. The vast majority of these items are proximally ground *Marginella* sp. shell beads recovered from the salvaged group burial on the

Table 10. Human osteological remains from the Powell Mound, arranged by gross provenience units.

PROVENIENCE	ELEMENT	NUMBER
Premound	Right half of mandible, I2, M2, and M3 present; M1 socket resorbed	1
	Frontal fragment	1
Depression fill	Occipital/parietal fragment, sutures closed	1
Mound matrix	Complete cranium with associated mandible	1*
100R16 (pit)	Left scapula coracoid process	1
100R12-100R13	Occipital fragment	1
Unknown	Lumbar (L3?) vertebra	1
	Sacrum with L4 and L5 fused	1
	Femur (? side) diaphysis fragments	2
	Parietal fragments	14
	Cut parietal fragment	1
	Left maxilla fragment, with M1 and M2	1
	Left maxilla fragment with M2	1
	Radius diaphysis fragment (? side)	1
	Ulna diaphysis fragment (? side)	1
	Clavicle (?) fragment	1
	Right scapula coracoid process	1
	Phalanx (hand)	1
	Tarsal navicular	1
	Metatarsal	1
	Premolars	2
	Mandibular molar	1
	TOTAL	37

* This cranium may be from a group burial at the interface between the major mound construction episodes (Episode 7). It was recovered by Titterington during initial razing of the mound.

Table 11. Unmodified nonhuman faunal remains from the Powell Mound.

TAXON	WITH PROVENIENCE	WITHOUT PROVENIENCE	TOTAL
Mammalia			
Odocoileus virginianus (deer)	10	113	123
Cervus elaphus (elk*)		3	3
Unidentified large mammal	18	191	209
Unidentified small mammal	3	4	7
Aves			
Meleagris gallopavo (turkey)		3	3
Unidentified bird	10	38	48
Osteichthys	2	1	3
Gastropoda	6		6
Pelecypoda	7	74	81
Total	56	427	483

* Items tentatively identified by size.

summit of the main pyramidal mound construction stage (construction episode 7, see above). These and other items were probably collected by Titterington during the razing. Table 12 describes the worked faunal remains by taxon and provenience.

It was hoped that the worked-shell items would correlate strongly with the premound pit provenience, which would lend support to the interpretation of the lithic assemblage from these units. No such definitive correlation was observed. Nonshell worked faunal remains indicate an emphasis on perforating tools. However, their association with the microdrill assemblage on a functional basis cannot be supported at this time.

Botanical Remains

In March 1931, 17 samples of botanical remains recovered from the rush line below the depression fill were sent to Melvin R. Gilmore at the University of Michigan Ethnobotanical Laboratory for identification (Table 13). All samples are apparently from units 100R12 and 100R13. The analysis confirmed the field interpretation of this area as a filled marshy swale, since many of the species identified are associated with this habitat type. More material from this filled marshy area is available for analysis. It is still enclosed in the original field bags. Few other plant remains were recovered, but some fragments of what appear to be nut meats (acorn?) are preserved in glue. The latter are from mound fill proveniences.

Table 12. Modified nonhuman faunal remains from the Powell Mound. Identification of gastropods was taken from 1931 field notes.

TAXON	PROVENIENCE	DESCRIPTION	NUMBER
Mammalia			
Unidentified	None	Ulna (?) awl	1
	"	Diaphysis splinter awl	1
	"	Unknown tool (?)	2
	"	Cut bones	2
	100R16 pit	Cut bone	1
Odocoileus Virginianus	None	Ulna awl	2
	Mound matrix	Ulna awl	2
	" "	Pelvis awl	1
	" "	Antler tine	1
	Depression fill	Ulna awl	2
Aves	None	Large diaphysis, cut	1
Gastropoda			
Marginella sp.	None	Proximally ground	4
	Mound matrix	Proximally ground	229[1]
Anculosa sp.	Premound	Laterally ground	1
Busycon sp.	None	Various fragments	26
	Mound matrix	Drilled flat disc beads	2[1]
	" "	Drilled elliptical beads	2[1]
	100R16 pit	Various fragments	11
Pelecypoda	None	Hole in center	4
	Depression fill	Hole in center	1
	100L1 pit	Hole in center	1
	Premound	Hole in center	1
		TOTAL	298

[1] Denotes items recovered by Titterington during initial Powell Mound razing.

DISCUSSION

This report was written to fulfill the need for a long-overdue descriptive report of the 1931 Powell Mound excavations. The methods used in the 1931 excavations, the general mound construction sequence as reconstructed from field notes, and the descriptions of the ceramic and lithic assemblages are all important to our understanding of the Cahokia site. Our interpretations are limited by the scarcity of provenience information and the questionable representativeness of the materials. Only a small portion of the surface area of the Powell Mound is represented, and the upper 30-35 feet (9.1-

Table 13. Botanical identifications from Powell Mound. Samples were recovered from the rush line at the bottom of the depression fill in units 100R13-100R16, at 9.0 and 10.0 feet (2.7 and 3.0 m) below datum. Samples were identified by Melvin R. Gilmore, Museum of Anthropology, University of Michigan, in 1931, and the species names reflect the 1931 taxonomic nomenclature.

SAMPLE NUMBER	RECOVERED ITEMS
1	*Polygonum pennsylvanicum* (knotweed) seeds
2	*Populus deltoides* (cottonwood) bast
3	*Populus deltoides* bast
4	*Populus deltoides* wood *Polygonum pennsylvanicum* seeds *Chenopodium leptophyllum* (goosefoot) seeds Unidentified grass seeds
5	*Populus deltoides* wood *Chenopodium leptophyllum* (?) seeds
6	Humus with no identifiable plant remains
7	*Polygonum pennsylvanicum* (?) seeds Grass or sedge leaves
8	Silt with imprint of unidentified plant stem
9	Silt with humus but no identifiable plant remains
10	Silt with imprint of unidentified plant stem Grass or sedge stems
11	*Populus deltoides* wood *Chenopodium leptophyllum* (?) seeds
12	Silt with imprint of decayed wood splinter
13	Silt with imprint of unidentified plant stem
14	Silt lump with no identifiable plant remains
15	Silt with decayed wood
16	Silt with no identifiable plant remains
17	Silt with imprint of unidentifiable plant stem

10.7 m) of the mound is not represented at all except as possible inclusions in lots without provenience. Despite these difficulties, a continuity of phases from Jarrot (FAI-270 Loyd phase) through Fairmount (Emergent Mississippian and Lohmann phases) to at least early Stirling is documented.

In terms of the general issues that we wished to address regarding earlier interpretations of this assemblage, it appears that more time depth is represented in the lower few feet of the Powell Mound occupation than originally thought. At least 200 and possibly 300 years of occupation are represented, covering at least three definable phases in the 1972 Cahokia ceramic chronology. The earliest occupation of the area seems to be associated with the Jarrot phase (FAI-270 Loyd phase) but is limited to a few sherds that may represent a sparse but generalized habitation occupation. After that period, there is an apparent shift in the function of the Powell Mound tract to more specialized nondomicilliary activities. There is fairly strong evidence to suggest that even the latest premound activities and the initial stages of mound construction involved specialized nondomicilliary activities that incorporated large segments of the Cahokia population.

The general geographic layout of the premound pits and the core mounds indicates that even at this early date, the Powell Mound tract was geographically consistent with at least some elements of the larger Cahokia site plan. Premound activities, depositional contexts, and specifics of mound construction episodes share strong similarities with other mounds at the Cahokia site. The ceramic assemblage indicates that the initial stages of mound construction took place in the Fairmount (or Lohmann) to early Stirling phases. This is also consistent with other temporal evidence of the onset of a major mound construction phase at Cahokia at this time (Fowler 1972, n.d.; Porter 1974). Of course, more detailed examination of the other collections from the Powell Mound area could greatly enhance these interpretations. It is hoped that with this initial descriptive report as stimulus, more detailed analyses will be forthcoming.

LITERATURE CITED

Ahler, Steven R.
1977 Functional Considerations of Mound 72 Projectile Points. Ms. on file, University of Wisconsin--Milwaukee Archaeological Research Laboratories.

Bareis, Charles J., and James W. Porter (editors)
1984 *American Bottom Archaeology--A Summary of the FAI-270 Project Contribution to the Culture History of the Mississippi River Valley.* University of Illinois Press, Urbana and Chicago.

Emerson, Thomas E. and Douglas K. Jackson
1984 *The BBB Motor Site (11-Ms-595).* American Bottom Archaeology FAI-270 Site Reports, Vol. 6. University of Illinois Press, Urbana and Chicago.

Fowler, Melvin L.
n.d. *Atlas of the Cahokia Site.* Ms. submitted to Illinois Department of Conservation, Springfield.

Fowler, Melvin L., and Robert L. Hall
1972 *Archaeological Phases at Cahokia.* Illinois State Museum Papers in Anthropology, No. 1. Springfield.

1975 *Archaeological Phases at Cahokia, in Perspectives in Cahokia Archaeology.* Illinois Archaeological Survey Bulletin No. 10, pp. 1-14. Urbana.

Gilmore, Melvin R.
n.d. Results from Examination of Samples of Earth from Powell Mound, Madison County, Illinois. Duplicated correspondence on file at the Illinois State Museum, Springfield.

Gregg, Michael
1975 *Settlement Morphology and Production Specialization: The Horseshoe Lake Site, A Case Study.* Ph.D. dissertation, Department of Anthropology, University of Wisconsin--Milwaukee.

Griffin, James B.
1949 The Cahokia Ceramic Complexes. In *Proceedings of the Fifth Plains Conference for* Archaeology, pp. 44-58. Notebook No. 1 of the Laboratory of Anthropology, University of Nebraska. Lincoln.

Griffin, James B., and Volney Jones
1977 The University of Michigan Excavations at the Pulcher Site in 1950. *American Antiquity* 42:462-488.

Ives, David L.
1975 *The Crescent Hills Prehistoric Quarrying Area.* Museum Brief No. 22, University of Missouri, Columbia.

Keeley, Lawrence H.
1980 *Experimental Determination of Stone Tool Uses.* University of Chicago Press. Chicago.

Kelley, A. R.
1933 Some Problems of Recent Cahokia Archaeology. *Transactions of the Illinois State Academy of Science,* 25:101-103. Springfield.

Kelley, A. R., and Fay-Cooper Cole
1931 Rediscovering Illinois. *Blue Book of the State of Illinois*, 1931-1932, pp. 328-334. Springfield.

Kelly, John E., Steven J. Ozak, Douglas K. Jackson, Dale L. McElrath, Fred A. Finney, and Duane Esarey
1984 Emergent Mississippian Period. In *American Bottom Archaeology: A summary of the FAI-270 Project Contribution to the Culture History of the Mississippi River Valley*, edited by C. J. Bareis and J. W. Porter, pp. 128-157. University of Illinois Press, Urbana.

Mason, Ronald J., and Gregory R. Perino
1961 Microblades at Cahokia, Illinois. *American Antiquity* 26:553-557.

Milner, George R.
1983 *The East St. Louis Stone Quarry Site Cemetery (11-S-468).* American Bottom Archaeology FAI-270 Site Reports, Vol. 1. University of Illinois Press, Urbana and Chicago.

Milner, George R. and Joyce A. Williams
1984 *The Julien site (11-S-63).* American Bottom Archaeology FAI-270 Site Reports, Vol 7. University of Illinois Press, Urbana and Chicago.

Milner, George R., Thomas E. Emerson, Mark W. Mehrer, Joyce A. Williams, and Duane Esarey
1984 Mississippian and Oneota Period. In *American Bottom Archaeology: A Summary of the FAI-270 Project Contribution to the Culture History of the Mississippi River Valley*, edited by C. J. Bareis and J. W. Porter, pp. 158-186. University of Illinois Press, Urbana.

Moorehead, Warren K.
1923 *The Cahokia Mounds: Part I, A Report of Progress* by Warren K. Moorehead, and *Part II, Some Geological Aspects* by Morris M. Leighton. University of Illinois Bulletin, Vol. 21, No. 6. Urbana.

1929 *The Cahokia Mounds*. University of Illinois Bulletin, Vol. 26, No. 4. Urbana.

Newcomer, M. H., and Lawrence H. Keeley
1979 Testing a Method of Microwear Analysis with Experimental Flint Tools. In *Lithic Use-Wear Analysis*, edited by B. M. Hayden, pp. 195-205. Academic Press, New York.

Perino, Gregory R.
1971 The Mississippian Component at the Schild Site (No. 4) Greene County, Illinois. In *Mississippian Site Archaeology in Illinois*, Volume 1. Illinois Archaeological Survey Bulletin No. 8, pp. 1-148.

Phillips, James, Robert Hall, and Richard W. Yerkes
1980 *Investigations at the Labras Lake Site*, Volume I, Archaeology. Department of Anthropology, University of Illinois at Chicago, Reports of Investigations 1.

Phillips, Phillip
1970 Archaeological Survey in the Lower Yazoo Basin, Mississippi, 1949-1955. *Papers of the Peabody Museum of Archaeology and Ethnology*, Vol. 60, Cambridge, Massachusetts.

Porter, James W.
1974 Cahokia Archaeology as Viewed from the Mitchell Site: A Satellite Community at A.D. 1150-1200. Ph.D. dissertation, Department of Anthropology, University of Wisconsin--Madison.

Titterington, Paul F.
1938 *The Cahokia Mound Group and its Village Site Material.* Private publication. St. Louis.

Van Noten, Francis, Daniel Cahen, and Lawrence Keeley
1980 A Paleolithic Campsite in Belgium. *Scientific American* 242:48-55.

Vander Leest, Barbara
1980 The Ramey Field, Cahokia, Surface Collection: A Functional Analysis of Spatial Structure. Ph.D. dissertation, University of Wisconsin--Milwaukee.

Vogel, Joseph O.
1975 Trends in Cahokia Ceramics: Preliminary Study of the Collections from Tracts 15A and 15B. In *Perspectives in Archaeology.* Illinois Archaeological Survey Bulletin No. 10, pp. 32-125. Urbana.

Yerkes, Richard W.
1983 Microwear, Microdrills, and Mississippian Craft Specialization. *American Antiquity* 48:499-518.

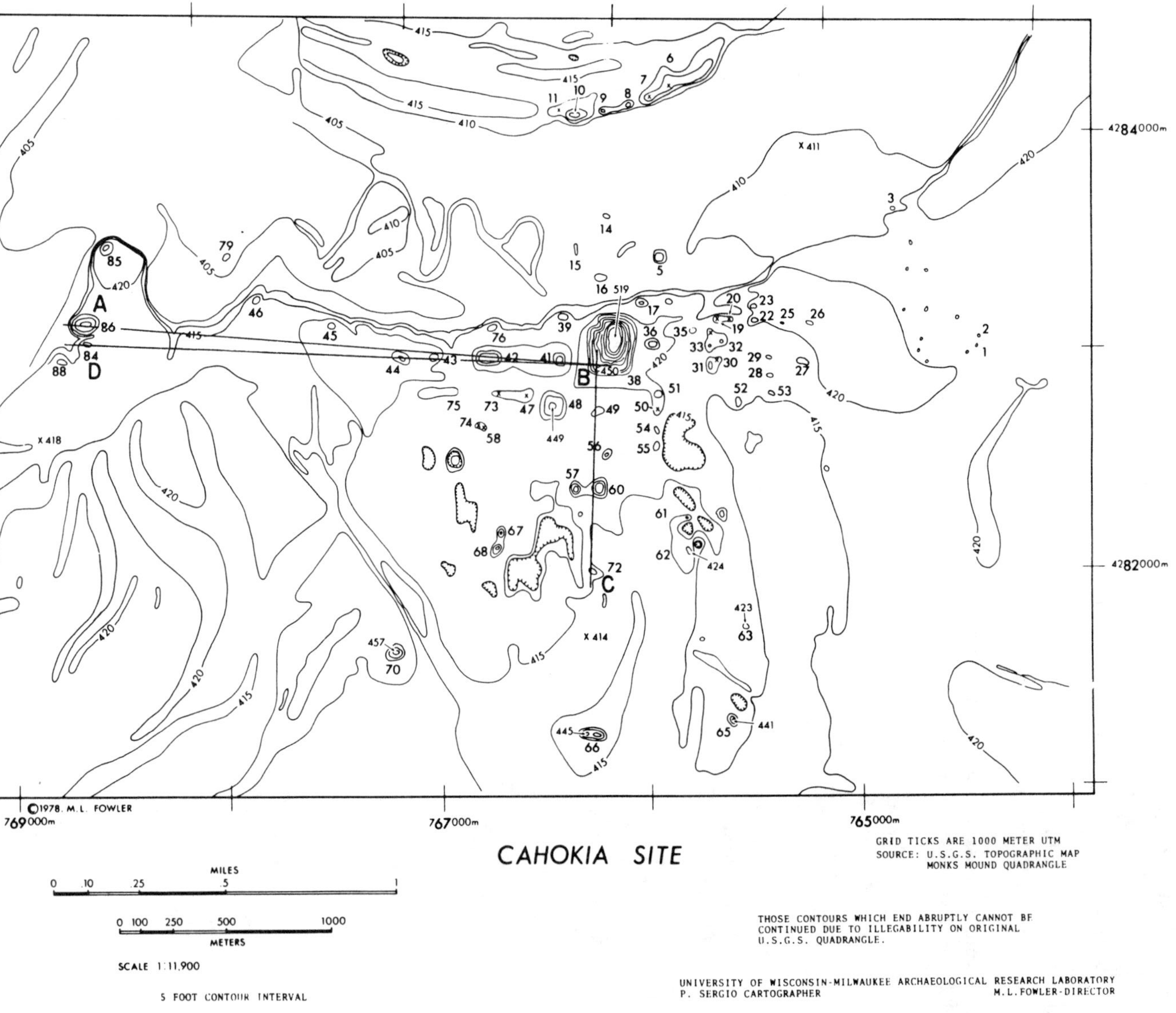

Figure 3. Location of the Powell Mound (A, number 86) in relation to other mounds at Cahokia. Location B is a low conical mound on the southwestern corner of the first terrace of Monks Mound; location C is Mound 72; Location D is Mound 84. Angle ABC is 92°; angle DBC is 90°. (Figure reproduced courtesy of University of Wisconsin--Milwaukee Archaeological Research Laboratories.)

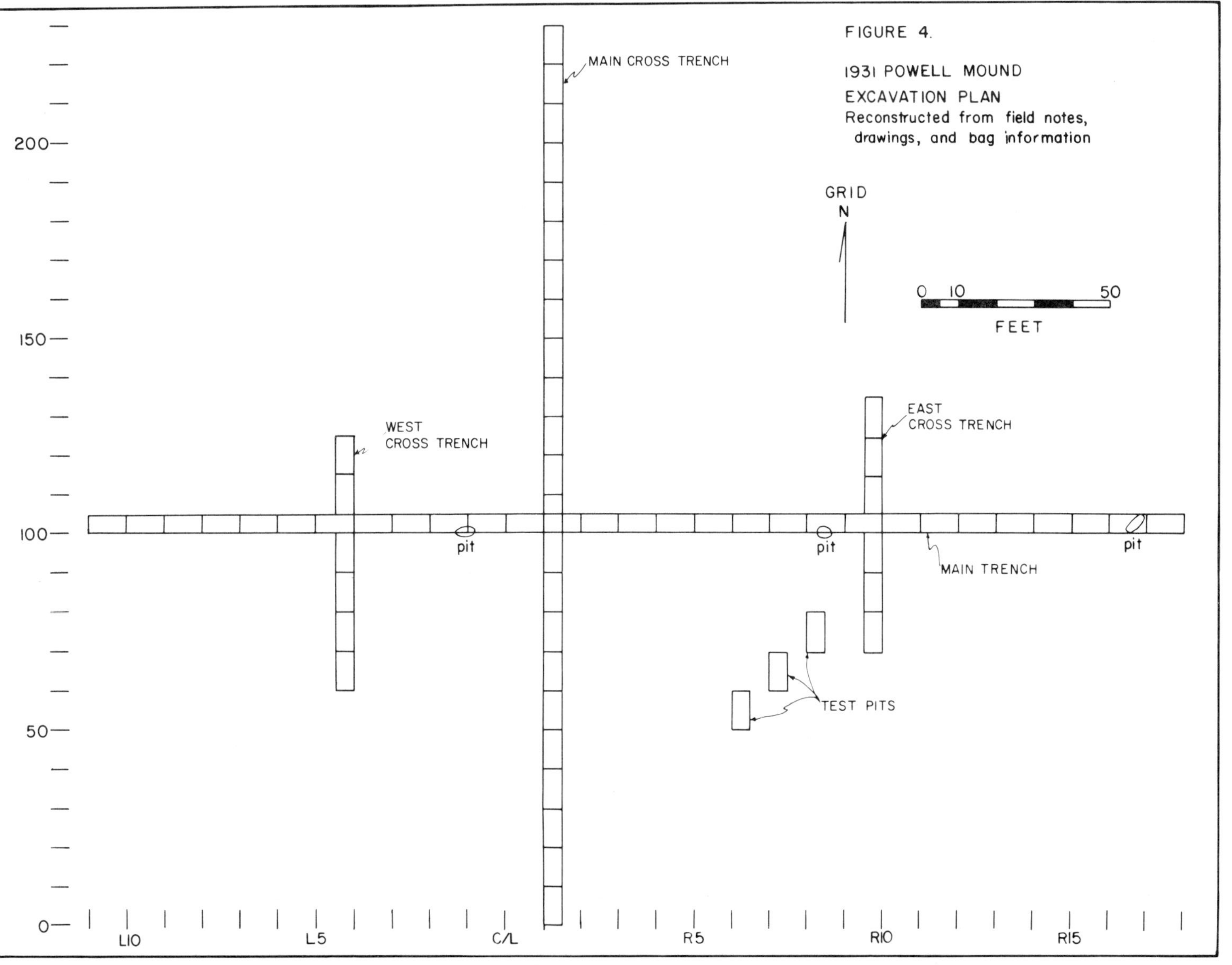

Figure 4. Reconstructed excavation plan for the University of Chicago controlled excavations at the base of Powell Mound.

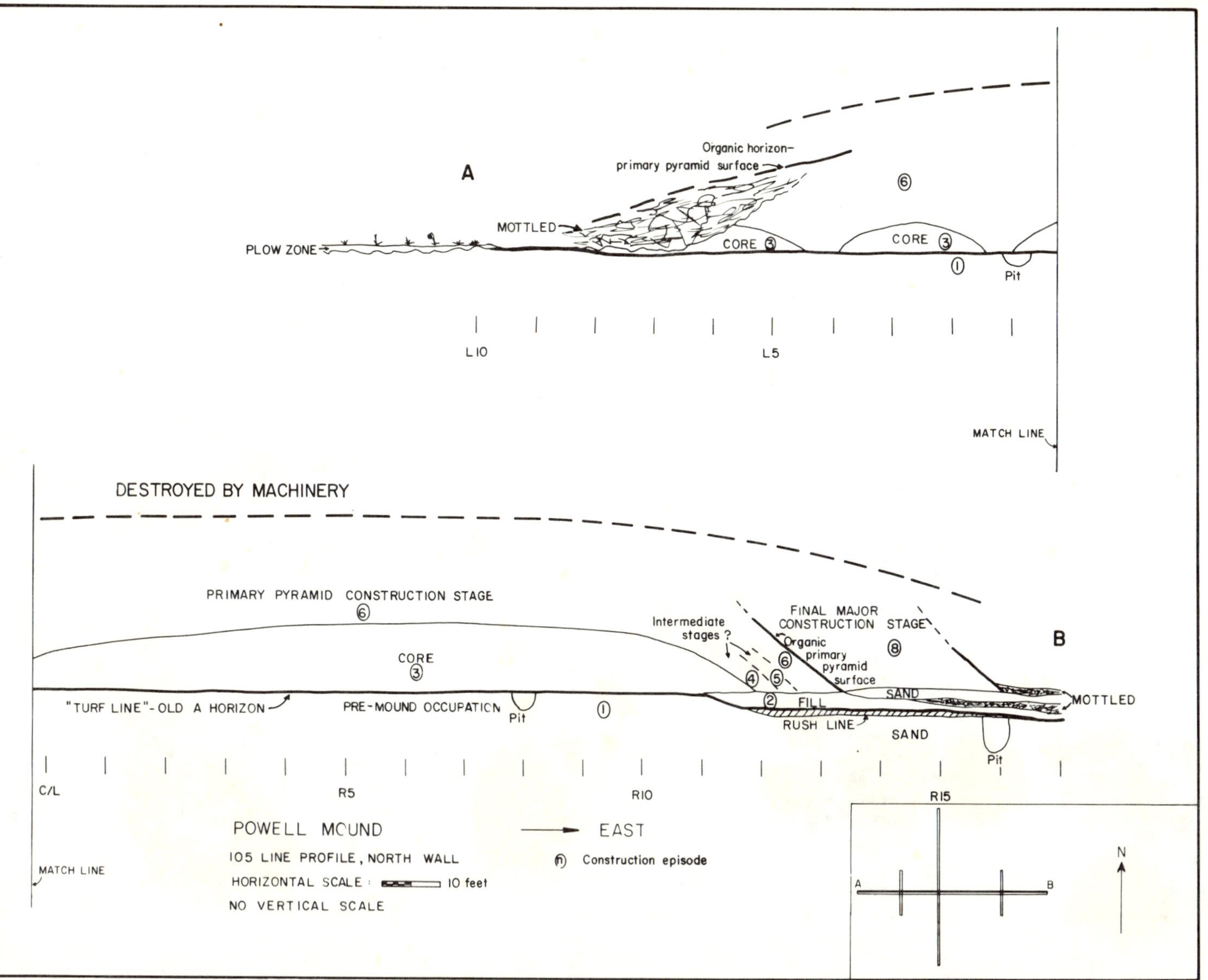

Figure 5. Reconstruction of the Main Trench east-west profile through the basal portion of the Powell Mound. Construction/activity episodes are numbered. The sources for the reconstruction information are field notes (Book #2), sketches, and bag lists.